D0743624

RECLAIMING STOLEN EARTH

An Africana Ecotheology

JAWANZA ERIC CLARK

ORBIS BOOKS
Maryknoll, New York

Founded in 1970, Orbis Books endeavors to publish works that enlighten the mind, nourish the spirit, and challenge the conscience. The publishing arm of the Maryknoll Fathers and Brothers, Orbis seeks to explore the global dimensions of the Christian faith and mission, to invite dialogue with diverse cultures and religious traditions, and to serve the cause of reconciliation and peace. The books published reflect the views of their authors and do not represent the official position of the Maryknoll Society. To learn more about Orbis Books, please visit our website at www.orbisbooks.com.

Copyright © 2022 by Jawanza Eric Clark

Published by Orbis Books, P.O. Box 302, Maryknoll, NY 10545-0302.

All rights reserved.

No part of this publication may be reproduced or transmitted in any form or by any means, electronic or mechanical, including photocopying, recording, or any information storage or retrieval system, without prior permission in writing from the publisher.

Queries regarding rights and permissions should be addressed to: Orbis Books, P.O. Box 302, Maryknoll, NY 10545-0302.

Manufactured in the United States of America

Library of Congress Cataloging-in-Publication Data

Names: Clark, Jawanza Eric, author.
Title: Reclaiming stolen earth : an Africana ecotheology / Jawanza
    Eric Clark.
Description: Maryknoll, NY : Orbis Books, [2022] | Includes
    bibliographical references and index. | Summary: "Argues that the
    problem of impending ecological devastation cannot be solved without
    a repudiation of whiteness, and white theology that created it"—Provided
    by publisher.
Identifiers: LCCN 2022022484 (print) | LCCN 2022022485
    (ebook) | ISBN 9781626984806 (trade paperback) | ISBN
    9781608339426 (epub)
Subjects: LCSH: Ecotheology—Africa.
Classification: LCC BT695.5 .C529 2022 (print) | LCC BT695.5
    (ebook) |
    DDC 261.8/8096—dc23/eng/20220623
LC record available at https://lccn.loc.gov/2022022484
LC ebook record available at https://lccn.loc.gov/2022022485

Contents

Acknowledgments

Writing a book is an arduous and frustrating endeavor. This one was particularly taxing, because it was written primarily during a global pandemic. The traditional structures of support were not available. Nevertheless, I was able to bring the project to fruition, and I am grateful to all those who contributed to the completion of this work. First, I would like to thank Manhattan College for providing me with financial support through two summer research grants and a sabbatical. Second, I want to thank all who offered support from afar during the periods of physical distancing and quarantine, particularly my mother, Yvonne Ragsdale, and my father, Isaac Clark Jr. But I am especially grateful to my wife, Jennifer "Miniya" Clark, who supported me even through her own vicious bout with Covid-19. She continues to be my greatest supporter, providing me with the encouragement to keep going in the midst of incredible episodes of isolation and despondency and offering insightful suggestions and food for thought. I am ever grateful. I hope this work is representative of the loving kindness poured into me by so many over the years. To God be the glory!

Introduction

Black liberation theology has radically innovated the discipline of theology and transformed its methodology. Coming on the heels of the civil rights and Black Power movements, Black theology offered a critique of mainstream Protestant theology's inability to address the problem of racism, the core foundation of American society. James Cone, Albert Cleage Jr., Gayraud Wilmore, and others argued that theology is not constructed from an objective and neutral location. Theologians are situated in a particular context, and Protestant white theology is incapable of addressing the problem of whiteness that lies at the core of the racial problem in America. American theologians like Reinhold Niebuhr are infected with whiteness; thus, their way of doing theology is not capable of establishing a basis for freeing oppressed Black people from racial oppression. Their theology is not objective or universal, as it claims to be. It is a white theology. For Black people to be free, theologians like Cone, Cleage, and Wilmore argue that Black Christians must be guided by a Black liberation theology deriving from the Black experience and rooted in a biblical hermeneutics that understands liberation as the main theme of the Bible.

Other forms of liberation theology have emerged since Black theology's inception. African, Native American, feminist, ecofeminist, Womanist, and queer theologies, among others, were all enabled by the original claim of Black theology that theology as a discipline cannot be developed from an objective, neutral space or universal perspective. Ecotheology, yet another late twentieth-century theology, attempts to place the ecological crisis at the center of human concerns and revamp the symbols, models, and metaphors of Christian theology so that they reflect the urgent need to save the Earth from ecological destruction. Ecotheology has sought to reimagine God, sin, Jesus Christ, and salvation in a way that is not anthropocentric (centered around human needs and concerns) and to reframe human existence as part of a larger ecosystem or cosmos in crisis. Ecotheologians often argue for a cosmocentric view, a view that relativizes humanity's importance and concerns within a larger interconnected cosmos. They propose a radical planetary agenda and provide a dire and much-needed perspective. It is my contention, however, that ecotheology is hampered in its ability to effectively address the planetary crisis, precisely because it views itself as positing a goal and agenda different from those of Black theology. The result of this is a failure to see that the problem of whiteness, the main issue Black theology exposes and seeks to eradicate, is also the problem at the heart of the ecological crisis. Thus, the agendas of both Black theology and ecotheology are not separate but related. An African-centered, or Africana, methodological approach to theology reveals the ways in which analysis and even the telos of Black theology actually have radical ecological implications. In this book, therefore, I posit the land/Earth as a theological symbol needed to bridge the agendas of those theologies concerned with race, class, gender, and ecological oppression.

I name this an Africana methodological approach to theology, and I frame it within a larger emerging field known as Africana religious studies, which seeks to increase our understanding of, and to affirm and appreciate the knowledge produced by, the religious cultures of African-descended peoples worldwide. This need was exposed by some early critics of Black theology, who questioned whether the discipline of theology itself, as practiced in the West, was capable of adequately uncovering or discerning the full Black religious experience, given the centrality and importance of African spirituality and Africa as a religious symbol. Charles Long questioned whether Eurocentric methodological tools could interpret Black religion. For him, incorporation of those tools made Black religion "opaque."[1] He accused most Black liberation theologians of approaching their task essentially as Christian apologists who too often view theology as equal to the task of explaining Western Christianity from a Black point of view. But Long argued that Black religion is not reducible to Christianity. Black religion has to account for the way it has been influenced by the traditional religions of West Africa.

Building on this critique, Dianne Stewart and Tracey Hucks argue for a "transdisciplinary agenda" for Africana religious studies to address the methodological inadequacies existing in multiple disciplines, not just theology.[2] A transdisciplinary approach would incorporate methodological tools and data gained from secular historians, ethnographers, and phenomenologists, among others, in an effort to enhance our ability to understand the spirituality and religions of African-descended peoples worldwide. To that end, I incorporate some of the work of secular historians, sociologists, and philosophers, and I have in previous works engaged in ethnography to help unearth African-centered modalities and idioms foreign to Western modes of theologizing. The discipline of phenomenology is particularly

1. Charles H. Long, *Significations: Signs, Symbols, and Images in the Interpretation of Religion* (Aurora, CO: The Davies Group, 1999), 204.
2. Dianne M. Stewart Diakité and Tracey E. Hucks, "Africana Religious Studies: Toward a Transdisciplinary Agenda in an Emerging Field," *Journal of Africana Religions* 1.1 (2013): 28–77.

relevant for the development of a spatially oriented theology, because such a theology prioritizes each present moment, as opposed to past events recorded in written texts, and our ability to be in right relationship with all the natural—visible and invisible—entities that occupy our current spaces.

Only by transcending disciplinary restrictions and boundaries can we hope to begin to make Black religion authentically transparent. An Africana methodological approach to theology incorporates new sources and reprioritizes others, like the Bible, once deemed primary in order to study God. This approach leads to a deeper interrogation of the God-symbol and challenges conventional ways of conceptualizing divinity. Finally, this approach endeavors to demonstrate the commonalities in the agenda and goals of Black liberation theology and ecotheology when the act of Africanizing/indigenizing space is the linchpin connecting them.

The Problem

In her ecotheology, Sallie McFague redefines the Christian view of sin as "the refusal to accept our place."[3] She explains it this way: "We are not sinners because we rebel against God or are unable to be sufficiently spiritual: our particular failing (closely related to our peculiar form of grandeur) is our unwillingness to stay in our place, to accept our proper limits so that other individuals of our species as well as other species can also have needed space."[4] This definition of sin is insightful in that it offers an unconventional, spatial conception of sin, yet it is a definition also simultaneously infected with whiteness.

---

3. Sallie McFague, *The Body of God: An Ecological Theology* (Minneapolis: Fortress Press, 1993), 112.

4. McFague, *Body of God*, 113.

While it is obvious that the "we" to which she refers is the human species, one might question whether referring to the human species broadly evinces part of the very problem she seeks to solve. It should be noted that within her explication of sin she does argue that humans have caused harm to other humans. In her description of the subsets of sin, McFague refers to the way humans live a lie in relationship to other humans. But even here she speaks generally, and thus abstractly. She writes, "The ecological sin is the refusal of the haves to share land and space with the have nots."[5] But who specifically are the haves and the have-nots, and what ideology undergirds and animates their perspective and behavior? Whiteness goes unnamed in her ecological understanding of sin and is thus allowed to invisibly infect and limit the ecotheological project.

The failure to maintain our proper place is not an affliction affecting the entirety of the human species. In fact, indigenous African and Native American worldviews are premised on the need to maintain a proper balance and harmony with the ecosphere. These are cultures that for centuries embraced the idea of harmonizing and balancing space, or being in right relationship with the other living species and the natural world. So the failure to maintain one's proper place is not a universal human ailment, as suggested by ecotheologians, but it is one way to describe the vicious legacy of white supremacy in America and even throughout the world. Whiteness is greed and selfishness in spatial terms, the hallmark of which has been the conquest of land and continued brutal dispossession of indigenous peoples from their portions of Earth. Spatial infringement, conquest, and control provide one way of framing the oppression of Black and other non-white human beings, revealing the great damage conflicts over space have done to the Earth.

5. McFague, *Body of God*, 117.

Racism in America, in particular, has always been about the desire to control, exclude, and surveil space(s). Kelly Brown Douglas defines whiteness as "the right to exclude."[6] By this she means that white privilege has functioned as the license to control, dominate, and occupy any and all spaces without being viewed with fear, suspicion, skepticism, or envy by others. Accompanying this right to exclude is the collective power to inflict rigid spatial confinement, containment, and surveillance of oppressed black, brown, and red peoples in America and other places throughout the world. The problem is that liberation theologies, typically informed by a temporal orientation, have failed to connect the agendas of Black liberation theology and ecotheology around confronting the problem of whiteness. This book makes an effort to do this by developing a theology that prioritizes spatial realities and centers on the task of indigenizing and/or Africanizing our present spaces.

First-generation Black theologian Albert B. Cleage Jr., influenced by Malcolm X and the Nation of Islam, called out the racist implications of Black Christians' continued worship of a white Christ and a white God. James Cone went further, describing white theology as the Antichrist and synonymous with the ideology of white supremacy.[7] However, it has not always been clear for Black theologians what the epistemological underpinnings of whiteness are, and how those underpinnings might inform not just a racial analysis but also analyses of class, gender, and even impending ecological destruction.

I posit *white epistemological hubris* as the term to describe the pernicious way whiteness operates both to oppress the racial

6. Kelly Brown Douglas, *Stand Your Ground: Black Bodies and the Justice of God* (Maryknoll, NY: Orbis Books, 2015), 41.

7. James H. Cone, *A Black Theology of Liberation* (Maryknoll, NY: Orbis Books, 1970), 6.

other, with Blackness as its chief opponent, and to simultaneously damage and eventually destroy the land/Earth. The foundational tenets of white epistemological hubris are the myth of objectivity, a false universalism, and a vicious individualism, all framed within a temporal orientation. The time-oriented framework is key, as it allows falsely universal and abstract ideas, particularly in theology, to carry weight, value, and influence over spatially relevant, concrete, and tangible conceptions geared toward impacting the present moment and space. The discipline of theology, and Black liberation theology specifically, is hampered by its own reliance on white epistemological hubris, particularly in its tendency to universalize its central theological claims. Thus, as Long contends, it engages in Christian apologetics and suffers a methodological problem. Ultimately, it cannot do what it proposes or achieve its objective of liberation for a specific group of people. As a result, I call for an innovative approach to theological method, one that embraces aspects of Native American and traditional African worldviews that emphasize a spatial orientation over a temporal one. This means reframing space, and land specifically, as a theological symbol; reconstructing our notion of God; addressing the failure resulting from an overreliance on traditional Christian symbols like the cross and the Bible; and finally reexamining the goal, or telos, of Black liberation theology, such that it includes the reclaiming of stolen land, or stolen spaces, and Africanizing/indigenizing them.

White epistemological hubris essentially is an arrogance of perception and a misunderstanding of the natural world and how human beings exist in relationship to each other and the rest of creation. It relies on a temporal orientation, which means that time is the governing category by which we measure human success. Liberalism's understanding of "progress" is maintained based on a preoccupation with linear time. Human existence is presumed to get better with time, or to progress, as improved scientific knowledge leads to technological innovation and advancement. Thus, what comes later is perceived to be better than what preceded it. Western society measures productivity according to time. Theories of knowledge, specifically Darwin's theory of evolution, are temporally oriented and dependent.

Technological advancement in a machine culture is the ultimate goal of a society that merges its temporal fixation with the myth of objectivity. The separation of a subject from its object and the idea that the subject can know the object in a neutral, pure way have had the same harmful impact on the racial other (the non-white, especially the Black) as they have on the land/Earth. Like certain human beings, the land/Earth was turned into an object, a commodity, for capital accumulation, material gain, and other hegemonic features. The commodification of Earth results in the failure to view it as a living reality, as a part of one large ecosphere. A vicious individualism, which gained preeminence as a result of the European Enlightenment, fuels hyper-competition between human beings stratified by race, gender, class, and sexuality, creating a zero-sum reality in which success for the other is perceived as a loss for the normative white male. Individual freedom is construed as a defense of white, male, Christian privilege and entitlement.

In this text, I chronicle instances of white lynch-mob violence and their resulting land dispossession and posit that such violent events were not just acts of racial terrorism and blatant disregard for Black existence. More than simply representations of Black social death, they are also unaccounted-for acts of violence to the Earth. White epistemological hubris evinces not only selfishness and greed but also a failure to admit the truth that subjugated communities have theological and ecological wisdom to share with Westerners. I link the legacy of racist Native American and Black land dispossession to the current problem of ecocide.

The problem of whiteness connects the fight for racial justice with the urgent need to save the Earth. Theology as a discipline, however, is incapable of speaking directly to concrete matters regarding racial oppression, because it veils whiteness, a specific cultural creation, under the guise of universalism. Christian theological symbols, particularly the Christian cross and the Bible as "Word of God," are believed not only to speak to the human condition but to offer salvific efficacy to all humanity. Universal application of these symbols hides the reality that, for oppressed people, identifying with the "heroes" of scripture and redemptive suffering has not changed the reality of racial oppression. Rather, these symbols have helped manifest double-consciousness consciousness and have often worked to exacerbate the empathy gulf and the construction of the Black person as the racial other, as well as widen the gap between racially oppressed Christians and those oppressed on the basis of class, gender, or sexuality. A false universalism is sheltered by a temporal orientation preventing theology from focusing on the urgency of the planet heating and burning around us now in our current spaces, and the problem that is the failure to keep our place is not recognized as a culturally specific issue. Whiteness continues functioning invisibly as a failure or flaw within the human species. It is never named; thus, solutions to the problem of impending ecological destruction continue to be framed within the temporal sphere as we race to create technological solutions. Theology as a discipline is particularly inhibited by its universal imperative. Culturally specific symbols masked as universal lure Black Christians into adopting other people's symbols and stories (i.e., the Jewish narrative of struggle in the Bible) as their own and failing to incorporate their own culturally relevant and specific symbols, idioms, or modalities in a potentially effective and useful way in their lived experiences.

Finally, reliance on a Western temporal orientation works to camouflage the deception at the heart of the myth of racial progress in America. The idea that Black people have made so much progress in the last four hundred years fails to wrestle or come to terms with what Orlando Patterson and now Afropessimists name as the constancy of Black social death, the legacy of slavery. For Afropessimists, blackness continues to be constitutive of slaveness and property. And whiteness demands Black suffering as intrinsic to its self-understanding. This fundamental American racial framework has not been altered or transformed since slavery. Thus, the election of the first Black president is not progress if it is followed by a vicious racist backlash, the need for a movement for Black lives to respond to racist police violence against Black persons, and the election of a white man whose ascendence to the presidency is fueled primarily by racism, white grievance, victimization, and overreaction to the first Black president. Yet Western liberalism's promotion of a temporal orientation enables the promotion of the rhetoric of progress, which assuages white guilt, avoids accountability for whiteness, and convinces Black people that some degree of racial reconciliation has occurred. Afropessimists help provide a metatheory for evaluating the ineffectiveness of traditional Protestant Christian symbols, like the cross and the Bible, exposing the reality of continued Black subjugation and enabling us to work to ensure Black survival.

Incorporation of African (and Native American) spirituality calls for honoring and reclaiming spaces around us—in effect Africanizing/indigenizing these spaces—which means affirming a pantheistic conception of the divine and viewing the land, the space, and the Earth as a living reality with which we are connected and interdependent. The land/Earth is the home of our ancestors, who remind us of the vitality of land/Earth and the need for accountability and ritual cleansing regarding its reclamation and healing. Native American theologian Vine Deloria Jr. called for a radical transformation of theological concepts and posited a change in the tools of analysis for explicating religious ideas. According to him,

> Spatial thinking requires that ethical systems be related directly to the physical world and real human situations, not abstract principles, are believed to be valid at all times and under all circumstances. One would project, therefore, that space must in a certain sense precede time as a consideration for thought. If time becomes our primary consideration, we never seem to arrive at the reality of our existence in places but instead are always directed to experiential and abstract interpretations rather than to the experiences themselves.[8]

Shifting from temporal to spatial thinking asks us to confront and face what has happened to indigenous and Black spaces in America and around the world. I present an examination of the history of land theft and dispossession, its accompanying rigid spatial confinement, and the inability to indigenize/Africanize those spaces of land/Earth, not just in America but also in Africa and elsewhere, that likely would have been subjected to ecologically efficacious and spiritually healthy and affirming engagement if they had not been stolen from the cultures previously inhabiting them.

---

8. Vine Deloria Jr., *God Is Red: A Native View of Religion* (New York: The Putnam Group, 1973), 72.

While land dispossession on the North American continent is first and foremost the history of the violent conquest of Native American lands, my context, as a constructive Black theologian, is the African American and African experience, and I will focus on African and African American land dispossession as a result of white supremacist actors. Yet the theological assessment, sources, and conclusions drawn are apropos of Native American spirituality because my proposal draws from a shared worldview of the sanctity of land/Earth. The shift to spatial thinking, first called for by Native American spiritualists/theologians, reveals a new framework for accessing what has been lost because of white, Western colonization and hegemony. The point is to show how the history of white supremacist violence and land theft in America and beyond demonstrates the need to merge the agendas of racial justice and ecological movements. Perhaps healing the Earth requires that we return to something former, a perspective subjugated and dismissed, and not simply move fast ahead along the same linear path of Western technological progress.

Building on Deloria's call for radical transformation of theological concepts, I argue for a pantheistic conception of God that reimagines, or re-presents, God as an amoral, non-agential energy, power, and force incarnating us and the spaces we occupy. Understanding how Godpower, divine energy, works allows us humans to have increased access to that power to work to bring about the good. Here I consider the thought of two pastor/theologians who, in an effort to Africanize their respective spaces in America and West Africa, reclaim an African mystical conception of God, one that connects the transatlantic experiences of African Americans with continental Africans. What results is a type of Pan-African theology of spatial reclamation in which God is the connective power, force, and energy bind-ing humans to each other and the rest of the created order in one interdependent ecosphere.

I then focus specifically on two traditional Christian symbols, the cross and the Bible, and attempt to unravel the way these symbols have too often been interpreted based on white epistemological hubris, making them ineffective symbols of liberation. The redemptive suffering of the cross and the Bible as "Word of God" evince the myth of objectivity and a false universalism.

Finally, I end by examining what liberation means for Black theology given this shift to spatial thinking. Is liberation merely an assessment of which political and economic system will best empower oppressed people? Is it a fight between capitalism, neoliberalism, and/or Marxism and democratic socialism? Or should we consider the land/Earth and its healing in our conceptualization of liberation? In this sense, liberation must be reimagined in a way requiring that we indigenize/Africanize the spaces people occupy throughout the world. *Reclaiming Stolen Earth* is a theological and philosophical reflection on the pressing need to consider how the problem of whiteness, specifically as manifested through white epistemological hubris, demands a merging of the agendas of Black theology and ecotheology by incorporating African and Native American spirituality to save us both from brutal antiblackness and impending ecological devastation.

The year 2019 marked the four-hundred-year anniversary of the start of the transatlantic slave trade in 1619 and the violent dislocation, spatial trauma, and cultural alienation of African people transported as commodities throughout the Western world. Additionally, 2019 was the year of return to Africa, spearheaded by the nation of Ghana, for African-descended people throughout the African diaspora, especially for African Americans. Ghana is the spiritual home of many diasporic Africans, in part because it houses many slave dungeons on its coast. Most African Americans have West and West Central African ancestry. Thus, Ghana's spiritual and political leaders called for African Americans specifically (but also other African-descended peoples) to come back to Africa and undergo rituals of spiritual healing and cultural reclamation and reconnection. It was a gesture of unity and solidarity, a reunion, performed to bridge the four-hundred-year spatial and geographical divide and deep spiritual alienation engineered by the European transatlantic slave trade, colonialism, and Western imperialism. In effect, dislocated Africans were asked to return to those slave dungeons and pass back through the "Door of No Return," in order to reconnect with something lost. As a result, many diasporic Africans returned not just to heal damaged spiritual wounds but as a symbolic act of geographical and spatial recovery. This book is intended as a continuation of that project; thus, I draw upon both African American and West African sources. The shift to spatial thinking is a theological reassessment of how focusing on the land/Earth can heal spatial, geographical, and theological alienation and simultaneously draw from the deep cultural wisdom and knowledge of African Americans and West African and Native American spirituality. Let the healing begin!

OUTLINE OF CHAPTERS

In chapter 1, I argue for an Africana theological method. This requires incorporating aspects of traditional African and Native American spirituality, primarily as it regards the shift from a temporally oriented conception of reality to a spatially oriented one. Building on the insight of Mary Daly, who asserted that Christian theology has an idolatrous relationship to method in its glorification of a past, static event, I argue that a spatial conception of reality demands that we do theology—without being distracted by the distant past or preparing for an unknown future—based on our experience of the natural world in the lived spaces we encounter in every present moment. The world we live in today and the spaces we currently occupy provide the canvas for this theology.

In this chapter, I examine the legacy of a Western temporal orientation to the traditional Christian theological method. Much of the debate in early twentieth-century Protestant Christian theology has to do with disagreements about how and to what extent God operates in time or in history. Liberal theology sought to explain God and God's actions through the medium of scientific inquiry and the insights of the European Enlightenment. Liberals tried to demystify the Bible and discern the essence of the gospel based solely on the ethics of Jesus Christ. Neo-orthodoxy reacts against the claims of liberalism, challenging whether God, and specifically the revelation of Jesus, can be explained simply as a historical event. These debates amount to a dispute about time and whether God and Jesus are bound by it the way other human beings are. The question of Jesus's divinity, for example, was ultimately decided based on whether Jesus was a contingent being or an eternal one.

An Africana theological method, however, asks that theology prioritize the present and the importance of being in right relationship with the spaces we occupy, including the natural world. Revelation is reconsidered, and the African conception of *living revelation* is prioritized over a single, historical revelation. Living revelations occur inside living, visible bodies in the spaces they occupy. These moments then confer sanctity, even holiness, onto these spaces, making particular sections of the land/ Earth spaces of revelation, a part of the one divine reality con-

necting us all. Western Christianity, a servant of white supremacy, has promoted the subjugation of indigenous cultures and
their perspectives and has also used traditional Christian doctrines to perpetuate a view of the land/Earth that has resulted
in its objectification and exploitation. An Africana theological
method argues for the recovery of a *conjurational spirituality*.
Conjure is a different mode of knowing that gleans truth from
the energy, materials, and power, seen and unseen, in spaces in
the natural world that promote healing, recovery, balance, and
harmony with the rest of creation.

Chapter 2 focuses on the history of African American and
African land dispossession. It begins with an explication of the
divergent views of land/Earth from a Western perspective, with
its emphasis on private property, and the traditional African and
Native American perspective, which views the land as a spiritual
reality home to spiritual entities like ancestors and other divine
emanations. When Africans were transported to America, they
brought Africa with them to the extent that they tried to "indi-
genize/Africanize" the spaces they inhabited. Africanizing American spaces was critical to their acculturation and conversion to
Western Christianity. During slavery, the ritual of the ring shout
inside praise houses and outside on land, often separate from the
slave owner and his family, represented actions taken to indigenize
the land, to Africanize American spaces. After Nat Turner's rebellion, however, racist white authority shut down these spaces and
began a process of rigid spatial confinement for Christian worship
in the balconies of white churches. These antebellum actions are
emblematic of the more pernicious practice of land dispossession
and spatial confinement in urban slums many Black people experienced postbellum during the Jim Crow era.

I chronicle examples of white lynch-mob violence and the
subsequent land theft to highlight the brutality, vicious cruelty,

individualism, and greed that motivated these attacks and also to showcase how failing to indigenize spaces of Earth had clear ecological ramifications. These pieces of Earth are reservoirs for violence and death, and the exploitation and objectification of land/Earth is an extension of the exploitation of Black bodies that previously resided on that Earth. There needs to be an accounting, a ritual cleansing, and a way to offer ecological repair for the violence and death stored on this land/Earth.

But this phenomenon is transatlantic. Land theft obviously occurred in Africa as a consequence of European imperialism. I cite Ghana and South Africa as two examples among many of virulent land theft and spatial confinement of native Africans. My choice to focus on Ghana, in particular, is based on the fact that it was the first nation to declare its independence from British colonizers in 1957, and Kwame Nkrumah emerged as a symbol of a new African leadership. His fight for a Pan-African States for the purposes of trade, with each African country owning and controlling the natural resources and means of production in their own countries, was feared and undermined by Western powers. Nkrumah's admonitions of neocolonialism in Africa provides a framework for demonstrating how corporate globalization and neoliberal practices desecrated and exported the resources from the land and impoverished the people.

The history of apartheid in South Africa provides the most glaring example of stolen Earth and rigid spatial containment of native Africans on homelands and townships. Yet even after the Black Consciousness Movement and the struggle to end apartheid, postemancipated South Africa continues to live under apartheid-like spatial configurations. Azania critical philosophy offers a response to the assumption of white settler entitlement, calling for a radical reframing and renaming of the land and space and who has a right to its control.

I end this chapter with a critique of ecotheologians' claim that Christians need a conversion to the Earth. I contend that this claim evinces white hubris and fails to consider that indigenous African and Native American perspectives were already Earth-centered prior to the conversion of these groups to Western Christianity. Also the language of conversion is replete with cultural hegemonic logic, given the legacy of Western Christian missionary use of this term as a tool to conquer and exert triumphalist claims over the native peoples they sought to convert. The rhetoric is informed by an arrogant, ethnocentric assumption that non-Western, non-Christian cultures have nothing to teach the Christian West. Such hubris is the very thing placing the Earth in peril. We do not all need a conversion to the Earth. Oppressed people need to reclaim stolen earth, to reconnect and rediscover what was lost. The recovery of stolen Earth and the restoration of subjugated knowledge(s) are crucial elements of ecological reparations and environmental recovery and healing.

Chapter 3 makes the argument that a shift to spatial thinking leads to theology promoting a pantheistic conception of God. The God of classical theism and classical Christology derive from a white, Western temporal orientation. Because Black theology continues to rely on aspects of these conceptions of the divine, I argue that it is infected with whiteness and manifests double-consciousness or second-sight.[9] Second-sight is particularly reflected in the circumscribed way Black theology developed its doctrine of God. Black theology has not sufficiently wrestled with its refusal to incorporate African spirituality and religions as a theological source and the extent to which it accepts the Western pejorative of African religions as fetish religion. Eboussi Boulaga claims that the overreliance on Western

9. Based on W. E. B Du Bois's definition of *double consciousness* in *The Souls of Black Folk* (Chicago: A. G. McClurg, 1903), 3.

theological assumptions and claims about God actually leads to the fetishism of Jesus as revelation and, by extension, the cross and the Bible. This is revealed particularly in the much-heralded claim that "God is on the side of the oppressed." Like William Jones, whose provocative questions to Black theology continue three decades later to go unanswered, I want to know: Where is the historical evidence for this claim? How is this claim reflective of Black people's lived experiences, their present reality and constant condition of Black social death? Are professional theologians precluded from offering alternative conceptions of the Christian God because of academic gatekeeping protocols demanded by the discipline in order to gain acceptance as a professional Christian theology?

Conversely, I present two pastor/theologians, Albert B. Cleage Jr. and Ishmael Tetteh, one African American and the other Ghanaian, who, through their efforts to address double-consciousness in their respective contexts, develop and preach a pantheistic conception of God based on their embrace of traditional African mysticism. They conceive of God as the creative power, energy, and force filling the universe. God is the power that not only enables life but creates the possibility for radical transformation of this life into various new forms. This is the God we must plug into to do what we, human beings, determine is the good. But God is an amoral, neutral power that does not express agency like human beings. Thus, God is not on the side of the oppressed any more than God is, or ever was, a white racist. The God of spatial thinking is the God that is ever present in and constitutive of the space(s) in us and all around us. According to Acts 17:28, "In God we live, move, and have our being" (New International Version). These creative intellectuals incorporate a conception of God bridging the spatial and geographical divide between continental and diasporic Africans. In so doing, they offer a theology capable of overcoming spiritual alienation and eradicating the double-consciousness existing among African-descended peoples, thus promoting Pan-African spiritual and spatial recovery.

Chapter 4 builds on the argument introduced in chapter 3 by interrogating the way two traditional, Protestant, Christian symbols, the cross and the Bible, have failed to help Black Christians fight against whiteness and defeat racism. My contention is that the theological symbol of "ancestor" is more pragmatic and useful in working toward liberation and is consistent with the dictates of a spatially oriented theology.

In this chapter, I engage the central claims of Afropessimism that blackness is "coterminous with slaveness" and is marked by *social death*.[10] Black social death is a condition of psychological acceptance (by both Black and white people) that Black life is characterized by excessive human suffering and disproportionate amounts of violence. The cross, as the central Christian theological symbol, only enhances Black social death in its fetishism of redemptive suffering. James Cone's analysis of the correlation between Black Christians' embrace of the cross of Jesus and their experience of lynchings, especially spectacle lynchings, during the Jim Crow era in America illuminates the problem of Black social death and the ineffectiveness of the cross in ameliorating the condition. Contemporary spectacle lynchings, like the much publicized executions of unarmed Black people by white police, and even vigilantes acting as defenders of whiteness, expose the theological paucity in theodicean claims suggesting that God always converts evil into good. To make this point, I highlight Barack Obama's eulogy at the funeral at Emanuel AME church in Charleston, South Carolina, for the nine Black victims of white supremacist violence. Acceptance of the cross as a central

10. Frank B. Wilderson III, *Afropessimism* (New York: Liveright, 2020).

Christian symbol actually stereotypes Black people as superhuman sufferers, exacerbating the empathy gulf existing between Black and white people in America.

In the later part of the chapter, I demonstrate how white epistemological hubris, particularly as expressed in the myth of objectivity, is implicit in the claim that the Bible is the *Word of God.* African-descended people have failed to read and interpret the Bible based on their own cultural biases. In a misguided attempt to read it "objectively," Black Christians have too often identified with the heroes of scripture and too often assigned innocence to the text under the rationalization that it is the "Word of God." As Itumeleng Mosala asserted, "oppressive texts can't be tamed and converted into liberating texts."[11] Randall Bailey proposes a *freedom of interpretation* for Black Christians if the Bible is to continue to serve as a source for their theologizing.[12] This Africana theological approach gestures toward a relegation of the Bible to a secondary source, and I posit the ancestor as a theological symbol that should be elevated above the Bible for this Africana ecotheology.

The fifth and final chapter focuses on the telos, or goal, of Black liberation theology. In effect, what does liberation mean and how will we know when we have achieved it? Cornel West's work took Black theology to task early on regarding its definition of liberation. He was particularly concerned that Black theology lacked an analysis of class and the political economy and did not possess an adequate social theory. West and Cone propose progressive Marxist analysis and democratic socialism as solutions to the greed and individualism endemic to capital-

11. Itumeleng J. Mosala, *Biblical Hermeneutics and Black Theology in South Africa* (Grand Rapids, MI: Eerdmans, 1989).

12. Randall Bailey, "The Danger of Ignoring One's Own Cultural Bias in Interpreting the Text," in *The Bible and Postcolonialism*, 1, ed. R.S. Sugirtharajah (Sheffield: Sheffield Academic Press, 1998), 73.

ism and neoliberalism. But a question remains if this definition of liberation is limited still by its anthropocentrism and silence about any political economy's impact on the natural world. Something is missing.

The analysis of Womanist theologians helps redefine liberation. They are suspicious that Black theology's description of liberation is inhibited by a Black androcentrism rooted in Black male victimization. They offer survival/improving the quality of life as the more appropriate telos for Womanist theology. Monica Coleman posits "creative transformation," or "making a way out of no way," as a new goal offering an alternative to the andro- and anthropocentric nature of the earlier conception.[13] Womanist and African ecofeminists open the door to consideration of the land/Earth in Black theology's definition of liberation. Liberation involves indigenizing the spaces around us, not just replacing the political economy, to create Black self-determination projects and, at the same time, heal the land/Earth upon which we all reside. I examine Black church and African-centered farm communities attempting to create such spaces. Ecological liberation ultimately is the destruction of whiteness, which finally puts human beings in right relationship with one another and restores and replenishes our one and only home, the Earth. But we must actively reclaim it!

13. Monica Coleman, *Making a Way out of No Way: A Womanist Theology* (Minneapolis: Fortress Press, 2008), 36.

1

In Search of an Africana Theological Method

Theologies of liberation have been innovative in large part due to their critique that the traditional theological method was narrow, provincial, and exclusionary. James Cone's Black theology of liberation argues that all theology is done from a particular sociohistorical location. Theology is not universal speech, but situated, sociolocated human speech about God. Cone's claim that what he was doing was in fact a Black theology exposed the reality that Protestant varieties of Christian theology before that point had always been *white* Christian theology. He then went on to vilify white theology as the Antichrist, essentially claiming that white theology is disingenuous, dishonest, and predicated on white oppression of black existence.[1] White male theologians are not transparent and forthright about admitting their situatedness and falsely presume to be able to speak universally. Cone exposed the epistemological hubris and delusion that lie at the core of *whiteness* in general (i.e., the ideology of white supremacy) and of white theology specifically.

Various marginalized groups have audaciously given voice to their experience of oppression by developing theologies that derive therefrom: Latin American, feminist, Womanist, Native

1. James H. Cone, *A Black Theology of Liberation* (Maryknoll, NY: Orbis Books, 1970), 6.

American, Mujerista, Asian, queer, ecofeminist, and so forth. Black feminist and Womanist scholars specifically contributed the category *intersectionality*, instructing us that certain oppressed groups suffer not merely from one dominant form of oppression but from multidimensional aspects of oppression. This was instructive because it made clear that one dominant form of oppression should not be analyzed and fought against in isolation from other forms of oppression. It took Black women to tell us that neither white supremacy nor patriarchy has exclusive dominance; they must be tackled together. In various ways, however, all of these theologies agree with Cone that the collective experience of the oppressed group in question constitutes a major source, if not the primary one, for doing theology. In this way, they all have a similar methodological approach and emphasis.

The problem of impending ecological catastrophe via climate change or ecocide, however, has presented itself as yet another concern that ecotheologians seek to address. Scholars like Sallie McFague, Rosemary Radford Ruether, Elizabeth Johnson, and Larry Rasmussen are ecotheologians and/or ethicists who argue that our ecological crisis requires us to reimagine our ways of doing theology. McFague posits that we must pursue a planetary agenda, an agenda that calls for theologians, even liberation theologians, to radically alter their approach to theology and also to incorporate new symbols. For example, she calls for a repudiation of the metaphor of GOD AS KING and its accompanying kingship rhetoric in favor of viewing the earth, and more broadly the universe, as the body of God. Accordingly, "our situation calls for a different way of conducting ourselves as theologians. Like all people we need, in both our personal and professional lives, to work for the well-being of our planet and all its creatures."[2]

2. Sallie McFague, "An Earthly Theological Agenda," in *Ecofeminism and the Sacred,* ed. Carol J. Adams (New York: Continuum, 1993), 86.

Ecotheologians frame the problem of our ecological crisis as a problem we as a species are responsible for. Whereas other theologies of liberation focus on the experience of a subset of the human species as a vantage point from which to make claims about all of humanity, ecotheology seeks a return to making universal claims about what *we* need to do in furtherance of this planetary agenda, and to even expand the "*we*" to include non-human creatures of the Earth. The problem, however, is that in moving too quickly to try to proclaim and implement a new planetary agenda, there is a failure to be accountable, which is rooted in the silence surrounding the question of how we got into this situation of ecological crisis in the first place. It is a failure to see that the problem of whiteness, the ideology of white supremacy, is a dominant form of oppression and also part and parcel of the ecological crisis. Whiteness repressed the indigenous knowledges of colonized black and red bodies which paid homage to the natural world and expressed a worldview that necessitated that human beings maintain balance and harmony with the rest of the created order. The repression, even destruction, of these thought systems in tandem with the radical dispossession and exploitation of the land these people maintained are contributing factors in our global ecological crisis. We cannot adequately address the problem of climate change, environmental destruction, and ecocide without exposing and eradicating the whiteness that created it.

Ecotheologians manifest this whiteness when they articulate an agenda for planetary recovery in a way that suggests that theologies seeking to expose and redress the history and legacy of white supremacy, while necessary, are somehow doing something different from what is called for by the ecological crisis. Their failure to see the intersection between the exploitation of the planet and the exploitation of specifically Black and other non-white bodies renders invisible the whiteness that lurks in the agenda of the ecological movement. What is required is a methodological shift that moves the locus of theology from the temporally oriented to the spatially oriented. Such a shift requires a reexamination of indigenous African peoples' religious ideas and concepts like *conjuration* and *fetishism*, and demands a redefining of mainstream Western categories like *revelation.*

In his essay "Whose Earth is it?," Cone highlights the racial bias in the ecological movement. He notes the tension between oppressed communities of color and white ecology, asking critical questions such as: "Whose problems define the priorities of the ecological movement? Whose suffering claims its attention? And do environmentalists care about poor people?"[3] Cone acknowledges the importance of ecologists sounding the alarm about the jeopardy we and our planet face. However, he also asks, "Do we have any reason to believe that the culture most responsible for the ecological crisis will also provide the moral and intellectual resources for the Earth's liberation?"[4] This question is important because it uncovers how whiteness functions invisibly within the ecological movement and among ecotheologians. The ease with which they adopt an agenda (which is not at all to speak to the legitimacy or pragmatic value of said agenda) that is then universalized without any acknowledgment of the subjugated knowledges indigenous Native American and African communities have to offer is characteristic of white epistemological hubris. Cone ends by asserting that "no one racial or national group has all the answers but all groups have something to contribute to the Earth's healing."[5]

---

3. James Cone, "Whose Earth Is It Anyway?," *CrossCurrents* 50.1/2 (2000): 43.

4. Cone, "Whose Earth Is It?," 43.

5. Cone, "Whose Earth Is It?," 44.

This book thus begins the construction of an Africana ecotheology that can make a contribution toward the Earth's healing. This chapter proposes a theological method for academic Black theology and Black church theologies that jettison a Eurocentric epistemology at the core of traditional Western theologizing and incorporate modes of understanding and knowledge derivative of indigenous African and Native American spirituality for a postmodern context, in order to reclaim lost spaces and restore, repair, and ritualize the sites of sacred memory of land and human bodies to facilitate the Earth's healing and reconciliation. Ecotheologians' planetary agenda must confront the brutal legacy of white supremacy by creating space for marginalized communities to offer concepts, idioms, and modalities in furtherance of the Earth's restoration. One way to begin this restoration is by developing a theological method that prioritizes a spatial understanding of reality, as opposed to a temporal understanding, and also rejects a Eurocentric epistemology in favor of an African-centered, "*holistic*" epistemology that values conjure as a "*divinatory epistemology*"[6] in order to access spiritual power in present space(s). This approach also calls for a reassessment of the category *fetish* as a term of religious meaning-making. I will unpack Black theology's alienation and unresolved tension with fetish religion in a later chapter.

Mary Daly coined the term *methodolatry* as a way to critique as idolatrous the traditional Christian theological method.[7] She draws from Paul Tillich's definition of idolatry in which he maintains that human beings construct symbols they then use to bridge the gap between themselves and God/Godself since

6. Charles H. Long, "Bodies in Time and the Healing of Spaces: Religion, Temporalities, and Health," in *The Collected Writings of Charles H. Long: Ellipsis . . .* (New York: Bloomsbury, 2018), 261–78.
7. Mary Daly, *Beyond God the Father: Toward a Philosophy of Women's Liberation* (Boston: Beacon Press, 1973).

God would otherwise be inaccessible. According to Tillich, nothing literal can be asserted about God beyond "the power of being, or Being-itself." The danger of religion, however, is the ease with which human symbols for God become conflated with Godself. This is what he calls idolatry.[8] Daly, building on a Tillichian definition of idolatry, argues both that women had been denied the right to name their own reality and that the traditional theological method precluded the possibility of constructing a theology for the women's movement because the Christian method required an unhealthy fixation, glorification, and elevation of a distant, deeply patriarchal past. She argues that the traditional, especially orthodox Catholic and Protestant, method reifies the past, particularly the central moment that marks the Christian historical revelation: the Jesus Christ event (specifically the incarnation, death, and resurrection). As Daly wondered, if that past is subsumed within a rigid patriarchal worldview and structure, then how do women in the twentieth century create new categories that speak to a new time and a new space, like the women's movement, if they are forced to speak of God only by reference to a slice of time in the patriarchal first century? This restriction precludes the possibility of asking new questions or raising new concerns in a new context. Daly argued,

> The tyranny of methodolatry hinders new discoveries. It prevents us from raising questions never asked before and from being illumined by ideas that do not fit into pre-established boxes or forms. The worshippers of Method have an effective way of handling data that does not fit into the Respectable Categories of Ques-

8. Paul Tillich, *Theology of Culture* (New York: Oxford University Press, 1964), 60.

tions and Answers. They simply classify it as nondata, thereby rendering it invisible.[9]

The *invisibilization* of this *nondata* (women's experiences) is, for her, illustrative of what makes the theological method idolatrous.

African-descended people know, perhaps more than any other group, however, about the ways that white religious authorities invisibilize and render as "nondata" spiritual realities, lived experiences, and theological constructs and modalities that do not fit neatly into "pre-established boxes and forms." Historically, traditional African spiritual modalities and technologies have been maligned and deemed primitive by Western religious discourse, as constituting a system of "nondata," through the use of pejorative terms such as *magic* and *superstition.* In furtherance of the subjugation of African spiritual modes, the traditional way of doing Christian theology has determined a two-thousand-year-old moment in time as exhaustive of how a twenty-first century Christian should process and make sense of the contours of God's concern and power. As a result, this methodology places severe restrictions on the theological imagination regarding how God might be working in the present in ways that do not reflect or derive from God's activity in the Jesus event or other biblical accounts or narratives.

Daly here is making a radical critique of theological method. When she writes about a "new time and a new space," she is calling for a reconceptualization of theological method that prioritizes our current time and honors the new feminist space the women's movement was trying to create. The reification of the Jesus-event and overreliance on the Bible as the record of this event are illustrative of the idolatry of method. Methodolatry

---

9. Daly, *Beyond God the Father,* 11.

then leads to a Christolatry and bibliolatry that are especially emblematic of Protestant theologies. Alternatively, she proposes a process that "involves the creation of new space, in which women are free to become who we are, in which there are real and significant alternatives to the prefabricated identities provided within the enclosed spaces of patriarchal institutions."[10] Her shift from a theology whose method is fixated on a past patriarchal time to one focused on reclaiming and reimagining our current space(s) is instructive and provides an important heuristic tool, as it pertains to the similarities in her methodology and the approach of indigenous perspectives being posited here.

It is necessary to note, however, that Daly's final constructive project is limited by her own complicity with whiteness in the failure to acknowledge the perspective of indigenous Native American and African communities that have long subscribed to the view of theological method that she presents as radical and innovative. In fact, her failure (and the failure of other white feminists) to be inclusive of the life experiences and perspectives of Black women is, in part, what resulted in the need to establish Black feminist and Womanist movements as categories independent of white feminism. In particular, Audre Lorde's "Letter to Mary Daly" passionately conveys Black feminist frustration with white feminists' racial and cultural blind spots.

That stated, the term *methodolatry* provides a useful concept for examining the shortcomings of certain Black liberation and Womanist theologies. The discipline of theology needs to be liberated from the methodological shackles that continue to ensnare it. Dianne Stewart Diakité and Tracey Hucks state this explicitly when they argue that the study of Africana religions

---

10. Daly, *Beyond God the Father*, 40.

requires the incorporation of "a transdisciplinary agenda."[11] By this they mean that individual disciplines, especially theology, are limited by the methods and tools appropriate to said discipline and the inability to transcend disciplinary boundaries and gatekeeping. Such circumscribed thinking limits our ability to appreciate the breadth and depth of knowledge produced within the religious cultures of African-descended peoples worldwide.

As it pertains to the work of the theologian, theological reflection and construction should not be limited to the traditional Western sources, nor should those sources be prioritized in the traditional ways. The Western Christian understanding of revelation, for example, particularly special revelation, has been critiqued by Stewart and others as foreclosing possibilities of explaining and legitimizing revelatory events/moments in the religious experiences of African people. Special revelation is the hallmark of white epistemological hubris. As part of the reimagining of theological method, I offer an alternative interpretation of revelation as informed by African American and indigenous African and Native American spirituality as more useful, relevant, and practical for addressing the urgency of the Earth's restoration.

A Spatial Conception in Theology

Indigenous African and Native American theologians/religionists have long argued that, while both Western culture and indigenous cultures are clearly informed by space and time considerations and limitations, Western culture prioritizes temporality, or a time-oriented conception of reality, whereas Afri-

---

11. Dianne M. Stewart Diakité and Tracey E. Hucks, "Africana Religious Studies: Toward a Transdisciplinary Agenda in an Emerging Field," *Journal of Africana Religions* 1.1 (2013): 28–77.

can and Native American worldviews prioritize spatiality. Vine Deloria laments that "Western European peoples have never learned to consider the nature of the world discerned from a spatial point of view."[12] What does this lack of learning have to do with theological method, and how might a spatial view of reality better confront the problem of whiteness and the ecological crisis?

Western culture's temporally oriented construction of society works well in furtherance of both technological advancement (or technocratic progress grounded in a strict rationality) and Eurocentrism (and/or the ideology of white supremacy). Native American theologians and activists have been making this argument for many years. George "Tink" Tinker, building on the work of Deloria, posits, "In Euro-American (and European) philosophical and theological history, it is most common to see intellectual reflections on the meaning of time, while it is far less common to see intellectual reflections on space. Hence, progress, history, development, evolution, become key notions that invade all academic discourse in the West, from science and economics to philosophy and theology."[13]

Making time primary has major implications for the construction and colonization of knowledge. Western secular, especially liberal, knowledge formations are rooted in the notion of *progress,* or movement toward a more progressive, advanced future. From Darwin's theory of evolution, or evolutionary biology, and the modern scientific method to Western liberal religious studies' assertion that religions develop and evolve from primitive religions to more evolved monotheistic traditions,

---

12. Vine Deloria Jr., *God Is Red: A Native View of Religion* (New York: Putnam Publishing Group, 1973), 62.

13. George E. "Tink" Tinker, *American Indian Liberation: A Theology of Sovereignty* (Maryknoll, NY: Orbis Books, 2008), 71.

Western culture is steeped in the idea of linear movement toward a better future, often predicated on some sort of idealized, pristine past. People are always in motion and feel the need to be in motion, often working toward something and in need of more and more. Productivity, especially in the economy, is measured temporally, in terms of how one uses time. This way of being places an emphasis on development and evaluates non-Western cultures by their perceived motivation or intention to be like the West and to mimic the West by innovating technologically, including excavating natural resources from the earth in furtherance of so-called human development. Malidoma Patrice Somé refers to this as the *machine culture,* and he makes the point that American society is characterized by speed. Americans never have enough *time* to accomplish their objectives. Somé notes, however, that "a more traditional look at motion, at speed, quickly reveals that speed is not necessarily so much a movement toward something as it is a movement away from something."[14] Constant movement can also serve to distract us. "And so the elder sees those in constant motion (going places, doing things, making noise) as moving away from something that they do not want to look at or moving away from something that others do not want them to look at."[15] What are Westerners afraid of seeing? And how has this temporal preoccupation, this motion, blinded and distracted us from maintaining harmony and achieving reconciliation with the world and the natural spaces we occupy?

For much of the nineteenth and twentieth centuries, theological debates regarding the relationship between philosophy and theology, between science and religion, and between historicity

---

14. Malidoma Patrice Somé, *Ritual: Power, Healing, and Community* (New York: Penguin Group, 1993), 16.

15. Somé, *Ritual*, 17.

and God's eternality all assumed a time-centered orientation. European liberal theology offered a corrective to orthodoxy by arguing that Christianity is historical and thus bound by space, but, more importantly, also by limitations and considerations of time. European liberal theology agreed with the conclusions of the European Enlightenment that elevated individual rationality and individual critical reasoning, and claimed that human knowledge from the past (such as the knowledge possessed by the biblical authors) was inferior to contemporary rational knowledge gained after the scientific revolution. Thus, science and theology do not have to be enemies, but scientific investigation and rationality can inform and correct the ways we demonstrate and practice Christian faith. This position undergirds Adolf von Harnack's concern with pulling back the husks of myth in the biblical narrative to discern kernels of truth in the gospel and discard nonscientific and irrational concepts like miracles.[16] He decided that the essence of the gospel was the ethics articulated in Jesus's Sermon on the Mount and the Golden Rule. These assumptions of liberalism are what led Rudolf Bultmann to outline a plan for "demythologizing the New Testament," stripping away the archaic, prescientific features of the New Testament.[17] But such "demythologization" rests on liberal, Western, modernist assumptions about what constitutes progress, advancement, and intellectual evolution and depends heavily on a rigid conception of rationality.

Of course, there was a European neo-orthodox backlash to the claims of European liberalism, regarding how time operates

16. Adolf von Harnack, *What Is Christianity?* (Philadelphia: Fortress Press, 1957).

17. Rudolph Bultmann, "New Testament and Mythology," in *New Testament and Mythology and Other Writings,* ed. Schubert M. Ogden (Philadelphia: Fortress Press, 1984), 43.

and the difference between human time and God's time. Karl Barth's claim that the Christ-event, specifically the resurrection, was an ahistorical event and thus not subject to scientific investigation placed the concept of revelation in a unique category that made it simultaneously historical and ahistorical. His metaphor of a tangent to a circle was a dispute about the difference between God's eternality and human historicity and the *once and for all* way in which those two realities come together briefly in the Jesus-event.[18]

Barth's description of revelation is particularly relevant, because it highlights neo-orthodoxy's fixation with describing God as *wholly other* than humanity, emphasizing that God is not bound by the temporal in the way that human beings are. Even orthodox Christology, or the doctrine of Jesus Christ, derives from a conflict about whether Christ is eternal, like God the Father, or a human being limited by his specific sociohistorical context. Is Jesus a son in the literal sense of linear, sequential order, meaning that he comes after the father? Christian theology that is derived from time-oriented suppositions produces a different type of God. It is a God of the alpha and the omega, a God of Calvinist predestination, and a God of the eschaton and the afterlife. God is in control of time yet transcends it, and humans are bound by time and forced to make the most of it.

Twentieth-century Western theological debates then create a duality, a binary between (1) those who trumpet human progress toward a bright future through a conflation of God's actions with the historically contingent, and (2) those who elevate, even deify, the past—the Christ-event, the Garden of Eden, and the exodus—as revelatory moments both historical

---

18. Karl Barth, *The Epistle to the Romans* (New York: Oxford University Press, 1968).

and ahistorical. Western theological debates essentially amount
to a fight about time: either the future, the rise and development of the West, the road ahead; or the past, pristine, revelatory moment(s) of God. We either look to the future or gaze
backward at the past. But when do we stop, in a Zen Buddhist
sense, to take stock of the present, the here and now, our current reality? When do we stop to evaluate the state of our rela-
tionships with what occupies our current spaces? What's left
out of this debate? What "nondata" is rendered invisible and
precluded from being a source of divine disclosure? It seems
little attention is paid to the defilement of the earth, the spaces
we currently occupy, and the defiling of Black human bodies
in furtherance of constant progress.

Indigenous perspectives ask, What would it mean to ground
a theology in the present moment, in the particular space(s) we
presently occupy? How has this fixation on time distracted or
blinded us from a proper theological assessment of, and engagement with, these space(s), including the land, living bodies
on the land, and the natural world? What are the theological
implications of the radical displacement and dispossession of
land and space that are the legacy of Western/European hegemony and white imperialism? Does whiteness promote a time-
oriented, abstract, (white) theology to further an agenda that
successfully distracts formerly colonized peoples from claiming
their rightful spaces by creating exclusionary spaces, or pockets
of exclusion on Earth? Whose Earth is it? Could a spatially oriented theology have produced a paradigm that radically altered
the trajectory of history and made us more ecologically responsible? How does whiteness work in tandem with a fixation on
the temporal? Black, Womanist, and ecotheologies need to have
a conversation with indigenous African and Native American
perspectives regarding the Christian theological method.

Reclaiming Revelation

I am positing the construction of a theology focused on revaluing certain bodies, reclaiming and reimagining the sacred nature of the space(s) we occupy, and, in so doing, restoring the land/Earth. The shift from a temporally oriented theology to one that is spatially oriented compels us to redefine traditional theological categories like revelation. Native American and African traditionalists have long argued for a different perspective and meaning of *revelation*. Western, white Christianity (white theology) is grounded in a historical revelation, a past moment. Thus, Christians are told to model themselves and to decipher notions of sin, redemption, and salvation through the lens of that past moment, that splice of time. The result is a theology that is looking perpetually backwards even as secular society marches toward an unknown future.

African traditionalists make clear that African spirituality prefers the notion of *living revelation.* According to Laurenti Magesa, "For them, revelation is a continuing and ever-present aspect of religious living."[19] God/spirit has the power to speak to and through any living being, including non-human creatures. Revelation is never exclusive to a single individual who apparently has some unique ability or access to the divine that the rest of us lack. Human creatures are believed to have access to the spirit world by way of dreams, bodily possession, manipulation of natural objects, or other forms of communion with the natural environment. God communicates through living creatures in natural habitats and living spaces where we live and breathe.

Similarly, Native American spirituality honors the natural spaces where revelatory communications occurred. "The places

19. Laurenti Magesa, *African Religion: The Moral Traditions of Abundant Life* (Maryknoll, NY: Orbis Books, 1997), 23.

where revelations were experienced were remembered and set aside as locations where, through rituals and ceremonies, the people could once again communicate with the spirits. Thousands of years of occupancy on their lands taught tribal peoples the sacred landscapes for which they were responsible and gradually the structure of ceremonial reality became clear."[20] This view of revelation calls us to account for our current surroundings and focuses our attention on the eternal now, which means that the present holds more significance and should be prioritized over the future and the distant past. Where are the places where revelation occurred and is occurring? Have we lost contact with and connection to those spaces? "Hence revelation was seen as a continuous process of adjustment to the natural surroundings and not as a specific message valid for all times and places."[21]

This shift in focus pushes us to reevaluate our space, the land, and our lack of reverence for the land upon which we reside. What gets exposed is not only the history of modern Western humanity's commoditization of nature, but also nature's defilement. It provides a lens through which we see how whiteness functions to monopolize and desecrate the space(s) all non-white people are supposed to occupy. We are led to redefine whiteness, as Womanist theologian Delores Williams states, as "the sin of defilement." This defilement is the violence, brutality, and rape conferred not only upon Black women's bodies but also upon the land and the natural resources of Earth. "The defilement of nature's body and black women's bodies is sin, since its occurrence denies that black women and nature are made in the image of God."[22]

    20. Deloria, *God Is Red,* 65.
    21. Deloria, *God Is Red*, 66.
    22. Delores Williams, "Sin, Nature, and Black Women's Bodies," in Adams, *Ecofeminism and the Sacred*, 29.

Womanist theologians help us move away from an abstract theology rooted in a temporal orientation to one concerned with the practical import of living bodies. It has provided a significant contribution to liberation theologies, specifically by pointing out the sexist, heterosexist, blind spots in Black theology's fixation on the evil of white supremacy. Yet some Womanist theologians continue to be hindered by an allegiance to a temporally oriented theology that relies too heavily on traditional theological sources, especially the Bible/scripture. In so doing, these theologians evince the way in which even some Black liberation and Womanist theologians are constricted by the Eurocentric construction of revelation and theology as a discipline. A *transdisciplinary agenda*, one that accentuates an African-centered epistemology, would help Black and Womanist theologies radically reconstruct themselves.

Kelly Brown Douglas's work *Stand Your Ground* is an aptly titled text to build on Cone's question: Whose Earth is it? In this text, Douglas deconstructs whiteness in a way that discloses the connection between the myth of Anglo-Saxon exceptionalism, whiteness, and the conquest of the land mass (portions of the Earth) that becomes the United States of America. She argues that the theology of white supremacy, which is tied to the notion of American exceptionalism, involves space and land, particularly the question of who is allowed to occupy which spaces. Drawing from Cheryl Harris, Douglas defines whiteness as "the right to exclude." She also refers to it as "cherished property."[23] She does this in the context of explaining how a "stand-your-ground" culture predicated on the suspicion of Black bodies in predominantly white spaces accounts, in part, for the rise in shooting deaths of unarmed Black men and

23. Kelly Brown Douglas, *Stand Your Ground: Black Bodies and the Justice of God* (Maryknoll, NY: Orbis Books, 2015), 40, 41.

women by law enforcement and pseudo–law enforcement, as in the case of Trayvon Martin. The "stand-your-ground" law is not only implicated in Martin's death, since the armed neighborhood patroller was emboldened to pursue him because of the law, but it also functions as a metonym for white power and white arrogance as it relates to the colonization and conquest of the ground, the land, and the space(s). *Stand Your Ground* speaks to the contestation about the ground and whose ground it is. Who is allowed and who is excluded? One of the hallmarks of the religion of whiteness is the conquest and, later, desecration of the land.

Douglas shows the theological connection between the whites (first the Anglo-Saxons), the land, and their belief in divine favor/chosenness. She notes that the Pilgrims and Puritans, religious radicals from England, appropriated the biblical narrative of the exodus as a basis for declaring America a new Israel, their promised land. The Native Americans then represented the Canaanites, the disposable people viewed as standing in the way of God's promise and as the people outside, the collateral damage, of the promises of God. They suffered a fate similar to that of the biblical Canaanites. The dispossession of the land of the Native Americans is not unrelated to our current problem of ecological crisis, but this is a point to which I will return. What Douglas brilliantly exposes, however, is the way the exodus narrative and Christ-event are used to construct a theology of American whiteness, white chosenness, rooted in the notion that Anglo-Saxons have divine favor bestowed upon them. Belief in that favor is the germ seed at the core of American exceptionalism. Whiteness is the *property*, the thing of value that manifests a corrosive sense of entitlement to all spaces in America with the divine right to exclude and/or express suspicion about "interlopers," meaning non-whites, and especially

Black people. At the heart of the problem of American whiteness, then, is the concept of divine favor justified and sanctioned in the Bible and the white Protestant Christian appropriation of specific biblical narratives, such as the exodus narrative.

Renita Weems warns feminist and Womanist biblical interpreters that critiques of patriarchy in the biblical text are insufficient if they fail to examine or critically assess the notion of Israel's election, which lies at the heart of the Bible itself.

> The premise here is simple: until criticism takes seriously the biblical peoples' pervasive belief in their election and their understanding of what it meant to be elected ("the people of God"), then we have not begun to resist the ideological foundations of the patriarchal world order, its ordering of society and its view of a select few in society in relation to the cosmos and the rest of the world.[24]

While Weems makes her argument out of a concern that the Bible is steeped in a patriarchal worldview, the same *problem of election*, or fixation with the idea of being chosen by God and therefore exceptional, is the issue that lies at the heart of the theology of whiteness, as Douglas makes clear.

The critiques made by Douglas and Weems, however, raise the question of whether Black and Womanist theologies are overly dependent on the biblical text, since they draw from the same narratives that promote a racial and gendered hierarchy. Do their critiques demand an epistemological shift regarding theological discourse? Even Douglas herself, after deftly analyzing and explaining the theological construction of Ameri-

---

24. Renita Weems, "Womanist Reflections on Biblical Hermeneutics," in *Black Theology: A Documentary History*, vol. 2: *1980–1992*, ed. James H. Cone and Gayraud S. Wilmore (Maryknoll, NY: Orbis Books, 1993), 221.

can whiteness and Anglo-Saxons' appropriation of the exodus narrative in her first chapter, then tells us in later chapters that the exodus narrative is central and indispensable to Black faith. She writes this after having presented Delores Williams's powerfully persuasive argument that Black theology has too long interpreted the exodus narrative as a single event of liberation instead of viewing it as a holistic story. In other words, according to Williams, Cone and others do not tell the whole story of the exodus. The whole story would involve wrestling with the problem of "victims making victims" of others in the name of God. Those who were oppressed in Egypt became oppressors in Canaan. Furthermore, Williams notes that it is unclear from reading the biblical text that God is not in favor of the perpetual oppression and exploitation of non-Jewish people, especially poor, non-Jewish women. Hagar, obviously, functions as a symbol of both the problem of surrogacy in the experiences of Black women and their invisibilization in society, theological circles, and the biblical text itself.[25]

Douglas responds to Williams's critique in a way that continues the trend of Black and Womanist theologies' continual reliance on the same biblical narratives that evince domination ideologies. Cone and Douglas often argue that Black faith (read Christian) is fundamentally different from white faith, and that the Black faith tradition's reliance on the exodus narrative has never been about domination and oppression but rather the opposite: a narrative of resistance. But Douglas never really addresses the full implications of Williams's critique regarding the Black faith traditions' consistent reliance on these texts. Douglas claims, "The Exodus story points to the fact ... that God chose the Israelites because they were a people in bond-

25. Delores S. Williams, *Sisters in the Wilderness: The Challenge of Womanist God-Talk* (Maryknoll, NY: Orbis Books, 1993).

age. The Israelites' particular historical circumstances serve as the historical context through which God reveals a universal concern for all people. The context itself is revelatory."[26] How can this be true given Williams's argument? We know what happens to the Canaanites. We know their genocide appears to be sanctioned by God. We know Hagar is neither liberated nor prioritized in God's grand plan for the Jews. In fact, in the Genesis text, God explicitly expressed favor for Sarai, the Jewish ancestor, over Hagar, the Egyptian. It seems that "the Israelites' particular historical circumstances" reveal a God who is concerned with Israel, their particular historical circumstances, and not much else. Upon what basis should we presume universal significance from this particular story except that revelation is perpetually invoked and has developed in Western Christendom to connote a universal category? Douglas continues, "To reiterate, it is through the particularity of the revelation of God that the universal meaning of God's freedom can be found."[27]

Douglas, however, concedes that "Williams is right," and Williams's analysis yields "troubling contradictions" about our ability to understand "the freedom of God." Yet Douglas's response appears to state that the contradictions highlight and emphasize God's freedom. It is worth quoting her at length here:

> Ironically as troubling as they [the contradictions] are, they point to the freedom of God. That God is free means the way God moves through history sometimes may elude human understanding. Thus, the freedom of God is a reminder that the claims we make about God may not always be about God. In this regard, the exodus paradoxes are a reminder that the reality of God is

26. Douglas, *Stand Your Ground,* 158.
27. Douglas, *Stand Your Ground,* 139.

always more complex and dynamic than our very faith
claims about God. If we are going to take the freedom
of God seriously, we must be reconciled to the fact that
we may not always know what God is doing in the
world. What must be trusted, however, is faith in the
knowledge that God creates and intends all people be
free.[28]

If Douglas is right and the exodus paradoxes make clear
that God is more complex and dynamic than our faith claims
about God, then why the insistence on ascribing to all people
the historical circumstances of a particular people from a specific, sociohistorical context that is over two thousand years
old? Why grant the biblical Jewish story universal applicabil-
ity, especially in the twenty-first century? It would seem we
should be circumspect and reluctant to overstate this story's
universal significance given the freedom and mystery of God.
However, categories like revelation bind us conceptually to the
claim that God's role in the historical events of the biblical
Jews do not apply just to them for that time, but to all people
for all time. This is a part of the methodolatry that hinders the
theological imagination, leading us to perpetually reference
old biblical narratives that fail to reflect racial/ethnic, gender, or sexual justice. It also continues the backward-looking
gaze and an elevation, even deification, of God's role in events
from the distant past. Furthermore, according to Douglas's
own argument, American white supremacism is tied to Anglo-
Saxon settler appropriation of this same biblical narrative. She
appears to be critical of white Christians' interpretation while
not raising significant concerns or suspicions about the narrative itself; thus, these theologians are allowed to fall back on

28. Douglas, *Stand Your Ground*, 162.

the thinly veiled justification that there is a difference between Black faith and white faith. But the Bible itself and Christian categories like revelation, which hold us captive to the text, appear to be sacrosanct.

Latin American ecofeminist Ivone Gebara claims that this problem is derivative of what she calls "an essentialist epistemology."[29] This idea posits that there is some preset notion of what the human ideal is and a requirement to conform to that ideal. "And these preset ideals are always rooted in the past—in times of yore, in some earlier moment of ahistorical purity, or in a given divine revelation—or else they are imagined in some blissful future, a final Parousia."[30] For Gebara, the essentialist epistemology requires inclusion of the biblical narrative, or some scripture, and results in the Jewish story being universalized such that it becomes everyone's story. For her,

> Essentialist epistemology recognizes that what is writ-ten in the Bible is expressed within a specific cultural context, but it assumes that it offers "something" that is above and beyond all cultures. And when we ask what that "something" above and beyond all cultures is, or how it can be apprehended by other cultures, or even how we can identify it as a divine reality, the answers we get no longer manifest logic or reason.[31]

Gebara calls for an epistemological shift, one that promotes a contextual, holistic, and affective epistemology. The holistic and affective epistemologies are key. The holistic epistemology "opens up the possibility of multiple ways of knowing what is to

---

29. Ivone Gebara, *Longing for Running Water: Ecofeminism and Liberation* (Minneapolis: Fortress Press, 1999), 32.

30. Gebara, *Longing for Running Water*, 32.

31. Gebara, *Longing for Running Water*, 33.

be known, of appealing to the diversity of cognitive capacities we have within us. These different capacities cannot be reduced to a single, rationalistic mode of discourse."[32] Equally important is that the affective epistemology she names repudiates the idea that cold, *objective* rationality is somehow superior to passionate, emotional involvement. She rightly notes that reason does not exist in a vacuum, completely separated from all the other aspects that make up the human person. "We are reason, emotion, passion, and allurement all wrapped up in one."[33] The interdependence of these human components is emblematic of the interdependence of human beings, other living creatures, and the rest of the natural world.

Gebara's critique of epistemology points in the direction of the subjugated epistemologies derivative of an indigenous African worldview. However, African-descended people in the West were encouraged to retreat from, give up, or dispense with African spiritual modalities alien to Eurocentric epistemological norms. This is the manifestation of double-consciousness, and the net effect has been conversion away from the African spiritual and theological heritage. Joseph Drexler-Dreis argues that even Black liberation theologies, and I would add Womanist ones, continue to be hindered by their reliance on Eurocentric epistemologies, which actually thwarts a realized liberation from whiteness. "Actualizing liberation in a meaningful way seems to require a liberation from Eurocentric loci of rationality, yet the means of moving toward liberation within theological forms of reflection often proceeds from precisely such a site— namely, from scripture and the theological reception of scripture dominated by the Mediterranean world and Europe."[34] He

32. Gebara, *Longing for Running Water*, 62.
33. Gebara, *Longing for Running Water*, 63.
34. Joseph Drexler-Dreis, "Theological Thinking and Eurocentric Epi-

argues that not just James Cone but other Black theologians, for example, J. Cameron Carter, express theological positions that depend on a Eurocentric conception of revelation. What makes it Eurocentric is the privileging, or elevation, of a single moment of divine revelation over every other possibility. This leads Drexler-Dreis to challenge the very category of revelation itself. He is right when he asserts that, "by relying on revelation as a form of knowledge that takes precedence over other ways of knowing, certain forms of Christian theology—even its liberationist forms—remain indebted to intellectual traditions that both legitimized and evolved within Western modernity."[35] He encourages theologians to seriously consider the methodological changes proposed by those in Africana religious studies. My question continues to be, What "other ways of knowing" lie dormant and subjugated within the rigid disciplinary restrictions and boundaries of Western theology? How might those other forms of knowing make a contribution to the urgency of the moment and our need to restore the Earth and the lost and decimated lands on the Earth?

THWARTING AFRICANA CONCEPTIONS OF SPACE AND LAND

My method is informed by the epistemological shift to which Gebara gestures, derived from an African-centered reassessment of space and the land upon which we exist. It calls for more attention to, even prioritization of, the present, as opposed to the distant past, particularly the present space(s) we currently occupy and the idea from indigenous African religions that we

---

stemologies: A Challenge to Theologians from within Africana Religious Studies," *Journal of Africana Religions* 6.1 (2018): 27–49, here 27.

35. Drexler-Dreis, "Theological Thinking and Eurocentric Epistemologies," 43.

can assess God in the eternal now of those spaces. It asks us to consider how God might be moving in the present moment, in the natural world in which we live and breathe. Are we in right relation with this/these space(s) around us? How do we restore the harmony and the balance, and honor God in the land, in the space? Traditional African and Native American spirituality has long argued that spiritual power manifests itself in the natural environment. Methodologically, this results in a difference in the current places where revelation can be found. These traditions reject the notion of revelation being singularly tied to a book, a written text, or a work of literacy, when the natural world holds just as much, if not more, of the mystery and complexity that are the hallmark of *the freedom of God*.

My methodology asks us to examine the racist and ethnocentric foundations and colonial legacies of both the study of history and the development of geography to analyze the current contours, the history of theft, and the misnaming of our current spaces and land. I am particularly concerned with the legacy and history of land dispossession regarding people of African and Native American descent. The descendants of the indigenous Americans, the pre-Americans, and enslaved and formerly enslaved African people have suffered vicious land dislocation, dispossession, and reallocation, forcing them to occupy fewer and fewer space(s) in America today. The history of this land dispossession is not unrelated to our current ecological crisis. The very people who viewed the land as sacred, who argued against the privatization of land as one's personal property, and who maintained a worldview opposed to the mechanization and objectification of the land and the exploitation of its natural resources, have had land stolen from them. This, coupled with a Christocentric and bibliocentric theological focus and orientation, has resulted in a certain theological alienation from the land as black, brown, and red peoples are forced to reside on less land in fewer and fewer spaces.

Black people are alienated from even their own spaces. This is not just a national problem but is part and parcel of the history of white Western imperialism. In South Africa today, even more than thirty years after the fall of apartheid, disputes about the land and about who has a right to occupy the land continue. The conflict is unresolved. White supremacy and European imperialism have always been about land and the control and exploitation of the natural resources of the land. Specifically, the goal has been to acquire the specific lands that black, brown, and red people occupy. This land reallocation is part of a larger narrative with ramifications for ecocide or impending ecological devastation. Focus on reprioritization of the space(s) potentially provides a new, yet old and historically subjugated, theological approach to help us better understand God and our relationship to God by way of the Earth.

Linda Tuhiwai Smith cogently demonstrates the relationship between land reallocation and the colonization of knowledge in her description of European colonization of the indigenous peoples of New Zealand. She argues that the globalization of Western knowledge, especially as established through colonial education, resulted in colonized people's acceptance of their indoctrination into new Western discourses, replete with new terms and concepts that transformed the spaces and reallocated the land around them. Smith contends,

> The globalization of knowledge and Western culture constantly reaffirms the West's view of itself as the centre of legitimate knowledge, the arbiter of what counts as knowledge and the source of "civilized" knowledge. This form of global knowledge is generally referred to as "universal" knowledge, available to all and not really

"owned" by anyone, that is, until non-Western scholars make claims to it.[36]

This presumed universal knowledge is reflected not only in theology but also in other academic disciplines, including sociology and anthropology. In non-Western countries, this "knowledge" provides the foundation for discourse about the need for these countries to "develop" (meaning become like Western nations). In so doing, "indigenous ways of knowing were excluded and marginalized. This happened to indigenous views about land, for example, through the forced imposition of individualized title, through taking land away for 'acts of rebellion,' and through redefining land as 'waste land' or 'empty land' and then taking it away."[37] Land displacement was used as an instrument to discipline, a mechanism of punishment. The colonized were disciplined by the colonizers in a way that resulted in the creation of enclosures. What Smith characterized as enclosures, the reconstitution of space, is identical to Douglas's description of American whiteness as *the right to exclude*. Who is allowed to occupy the space(s) on the Earth? Those who control the space also control access to space. "This is the other side of exclusion in that margins are enclosures: reserved lands are enclosures, schools enclose, but in order to enclose they also exclude, there is something on the outside. Discipline is also partitioned, individuals separated and space compartmentalized."[38]

This partitioning and compartmentalizing of space owing to global Western imperialism have implications and consequences for our current planetary reality. Colonized people have been forced off their lands, and that has had a tremendous impact on

36. Linda Tuhiwai Smith, *Decolonizing Methodologies: Research and Indigenous Peoples* (London: Zed Books, 1999), 63.

37. Smith, *Decolonizing Methodologies,* 69.

38. Smith, *Decolonizing Methodologies,* 69.

the treatment of those lands. This repartitioning also had a critical effect on certain species, some of which became extinct, and specific ecologies. Smith describes this as *ecological imperialism*, which also involves the intentional use of bacterial diseases to decimate entire populations of indigenous peoples.[39] The land dispossession and resulting mechanization and objectification of that land are achieved primarily through the legitimation of Western knowledge to subjugate and render inferior indigenous ways of knowing and being, indigenous ways of discerning truth as it relates to the human being's relationship to the Earth. This is clearly what happens to Black people in America.

Historically, African-descended people in the Western hemisphere drew from an indigenous African spiritual tradition that expressed a spatially oriented religiosity that placed great value on communication with God/the spirits, or discerning divine revelation, in the present moment within the present space(s). It was believed that divine power could be accessed in the present space, not through reflection on a past event long ago. This spatially oriented modality of spiritual expression paid homage to the contemporaneous natural spaces, and to all the visible and invisible beings who occupied those spaces. Yet this modality was vilified through a constant and tedious process of denigration and disparagement by both whites and middle-class, colonially educated Blacks. African-descended people converted over time to a Eurocentric theological paradigm that has worked in tandem with, and is not unrelated to, the dispossession of Black-owned lands.

Enslaved Africans in America initially mocked as ridiculous the notion that God could be confined to or subsumed within a book called the Bible. They believed that God is everywhere in the natural world; thus, receptivity to divine revelation does

---

39. Smith, *Decolonizing Methodologies*, 71.

not require literacy. However, the legacy of white oppression of Black bodies in America, including episodes of brutal, racist violence during and after chattel slavery, found justification in the white denigration of Black religion. The condemnation of Black religion was used as synecdoche for the immorality of all Black people. Charges that Black religion is nothing but "heathenism," "African savagery," "fetish religion," or "superstitious nonsense" are a part of the discourse of destruction, or what Jon Butler calls the "African spiritual holocaust."[40] Curtis Evans describes this as part of the burden of Black religion. Black religion is shaped by and constantly made to respond to the disparaging white gaze. Particularly after the Civil War, aspects of Black religion most alien to white authority figures were used as a basis for impugning Black peoples' character and denying them access to full citizenship. Accordingly, "superstitions, which meant religious practices of an African heritage, were criticized by whites as antithetical to a normative true Christianity and often their presence raised doubts about blacks' fitness to be incorporated as active citizens in the new nation."[41] The "emotionalism" of their religious rituals and services was tied to their presumed immorality. "Both white northerners and southerners also agreed that the nature of their religion made blacks totally unfit for labor, the central quality for freedom deemed necessary for participation in the new nation."[42] This denigration of Black religion was used as justification to refuse Blacks their full rights of citizenship, including the right to vote and the right to own and possess land. "As blacks lost their right to vote, were thrust off their property

40. Jon Butler, *Awash in a Sea of Faith: Christianizing the American People* (Cambridge, MA: Harvard University Press, 1990), 130.
41. Curtis Evans, *The Burden of Black Religion* (New York: Oxford University Press, 2008), 74.
42. Evans, *Burden of Black Religion*, 77.

to make way for white owners, suffered at the hands of lynch mobs, and lost any significant political and economic power in the South, white Southerners justified these developments by arguing that it was a defective African nature that explained the worsening situation of blacks in the South."[43]

My approach calls for taking account of the vicious legacy of white supremacy through the revaluation of the spaces lost especially as a result of white lynch mobs. How many Black bodies were defiled and desecrated on lands eventually stolen from Black owners? These sites of suffering are places of revelation that deserve memorializing, of ancestors whose memories should not be forgotten and whose energies continue to cry out from the Earth. That energy is a small part of the larger energy field of influence that African people once knew how to channel and access in their present spaces. To reclaim and restore the land requires an epistemological shift that includes reclamation of certain African-centered ways of knowing and being.

Reclaiming Africana Theological Conceptions

This chapter asks us to consider a theological method that performs an epistemological shift away from a Eurocentric epistemology and is based on a spatially oriented conception of reality. To that end, Black and Womanist theologies need new categories, or a radical reappraisal of old, dismissed categories, that can expand the conceptual frame for understanding God and honoring indigenous knowledge and methodologies. *Conjure* constitutes a category of knowing, or discerning, and a technique of communication with the spiritual realm that belies a Eurocentric epistemology or white, Western worldview. As Charles

43. Evans, *Burden of Black Religion*, 80.

Long makes clear, "Conjure is a practice. It is a divinatory epistemology and a deciphering process."[44] Conjure is a traditional African modality that confounds the Western, Platonic binary between the natural and supernatural, the secular world and the sacred. It represents a different way of knowing rendered inferior by the white perspective but illustrative of an orientation that reveres the space and the entities in the natural world that constitute that space. Long states,

> Conjure was theoretical and practical. In many cases it involved a precise knowledge of the effect of plants, herbs, and other potions on the body. The conjurer was also an adept social psychologist, able to read the moods of [slave] owners as well as the enslaved. The conjurer acted to provide so-called medicine for the body physical and the body social.[45]

I am interested in the connection between conjuration and the human connection to the natural world. How does conjure function as a category to disclose the symbiosis between human need and desire and access to spiritual power through natural phenomena?

The category of conjure evokes a reassessment of knowledge construction more akin to Ivone Gebara's holistic and affective epistemology. It calls for a radical revaluation of space and decimates the Platonic, Christian binary between the secular and the sacred. It connotes a way to utilize spaces and natural resources or entities in those spaces to decipher spiritual reali-

---

44. Charles Long, "Bodies in Time and the Healing of Spaces: Religion, Temporalities, and Health," in *Faith, Health, and Healing in African American Life*, ed. Stephanie Y. Mitchem and Emilie M. Townes (Westport, CT: Praeger, 2008), 43.

45. Long, "Bodies in Time and the Healing of Spaces," 44.

ties, to discern things, "*to see*" and "*to know*." It connotes an understanding of the Earth, the natural world, as the visible embodiment of the world of spirit in the same spatiotemporal sphere divided only by that which can be seen and that which cannot, or the visible and invisible realms.

African Americans have a long, mostly secret and unacknowledged history of practicing conjuring techniques. Yvonne Chireau provides an in-depth analysis of this history of conjure among African Americans. She carefully examines the practices of conjure as an African retention, or vestige of the African religious heritage, that became interspersed within the practice of Christianity, especially in the eighteenth and nineteenth centuries, and exhibited incredible resilience among Black folk traditions despite the virulently anti-African, American religious environment in which it was practiced.

Throughout the work, Chireau wrestles with the Western-constructed delineation between "magic" and "religion." She claims that, from a white, Western perspective, African-descended practices like conjure constitute magic, which is usually presented in opposition to the legitimized practice of religion and therefore maligned. "Magic" involves superstition and is often reduced to a private matter in furtherance of a personal agenda, whereas religion is a communal expression of devotion to God. This lexicon is problematic, though, because it falsely creates a distinction without a difference relative to much of African American folk religiosity. Chireau contends,

> What came to be seen as "magic" for the Africans who lived in America appears to have actually been a fusion of ideas that derived, in part, from older indigenous African religious concepts and the New World perspectives to which they were linked. Thus … a sharp delineation between "magic" and "religion" can be mis-

leading, for these notions were nearly always connected in practice.[46]

Importantly, "magic" constitutes a modality that resists Western/Eurocentric exclusive reliance on rationalism.

Conjure is a category that blurs or collapses the artificial distinction between magic and religion that typically connotes an anti-African posture in Western culture. Nevertheless, its resilience within Black folk culture compels us to examine it as a category of meaning that evinces a spirituality valuing the notion that the divine can be accessed in the present moment, in the present space, and by way of the natural world in a way that has implications for the restoration of the Earth. Theophus H. Smith proclaimed that Black people have often operated from a "conjurational mode of spirituality,"[47] asserting that African-descended people's emphasis on orality, specifically though not exclusively through the preached word, amounts to a type of "prophetic incantation: as religious expression intended to induce, summon, or conjure the divine for the realization of some emancipatory future."[48] Conjure is an activity, a procedure that invites us to think about the way the visible and invisible realms coalesce, intertwine, and are interdependent. It gestures toward the idea that spiritual power, or divine energy, is a neutral force that can be accessed and harnessed for healing or harm, depending on the intentions of the human actors involved. It involves the use of natural or created material objects, such as plants, charms, amulets, talismans, hair, nails, and so forth.

---

46. Yvonne Patricia Chireau, *Black Magic: Religion and the African American Conjuring Tradition* (Berkeley: University of California Press, 2003), 39.

47. Theophus H. Smith, *Conjuring Culture: Biblical Foundations of Black America* (New York: Oxford University Press, 1994), 59.

48. Smith, *Conjuring Culture*, 59.

Beyond this traditional understanding of "conjure" derived from indigenous African religions, I want not only to invoke its use as a reminder of the richness of the indigenous African religious heritage but also to emphasize the need to spiritually reclaim and divinely restore Black space(s). This category functions to disclose an African mystical conception of God, a conception not generally operative within Black churches or Black theology today, and is potentially useful as a conception for performing the human work of restoring balance and order to the Earth and reclaiming lost spaces. In other words, conjure invites us to think of God, or divine power, outside the prescribed Western theological frameworks.

The God of a "conjurational spirituality" is not a Supreme Being beyond the clouds but a symbol of a field of influence, an energy, breath, and power to which all energy beings, human and nonhuman, have access. Conjure provides a category of meaning that helps us transcend the limited and static conception of historical revelation, or special revelation, in favor of an active divine revealing. Instead of gazing back at some past pristine moment when God communicated a message to some special individual (or became incarnate in him), human beings in their own current time and space can create an energy field of influence and power that they themselves can access. They can conjure divine energy, healing, and power and, in so doing, also conjure social transformation, liberation, and ecological restoration.

Conjure points toward an inclusive epistemology because it represents reciprocity and interdependence. It speaks to the power to make things happen in any present moment without reliance on a past model or ideal. It prevents the circumscription of religious knowledge to outdated theological categories, specifically the cross, redemptive suffering, sacrifice, or ontological blackness, by opening space for new knowing and new *not*-knowing. Conjuration restores the mystery of God, even the freedom of God, to go beyond the categories of meaning to which we often limit God because we have absolutized a flawed God-symbol. Additionally, according to Long, conjuring is "not only a technique of healing but equally … an epistemology and a hermeneutic of remembering."[49]

Finally, this category reminds us that the Black body is part of the natural world and is therefore also a site of memory along with the natural world. Thus, conjure conveys the interconnectedness between Black bodies and pieces and places of Earth as sites of sacred memory in need of restoration. It is to the history and legacy of this stolen Earth that I now turn in the hopes of reestablishing the land/Earth as a crucial theological symbol.

49. Long, "Bodies in Time and the Healing of Spaces," 51.

2

The Failure to Indigenize Space: The Legacy of Stolen Earth

This chapter examines the theological significance of the land/ Earth given our shift to a spatial orientation, specifically as it relates to the long history of land dispossession and land theft that African-descended people and other non-whites have suffered at the hands of white imperialists, which is the hallmark of the modern era. It is my contention that the history of this vicious land theft must be examined in the current context of impending ecological devastation, precisely because this history connects the continuing struggle against the ideology of white supremacy with the struggle against ecocide, or ecological destruction. I will examine this history through a theological lens. How should we understand the land/Earth and its exploitation from the perspective of Black liberation theology?

Africans and Native Americans espoused a different worldview and a different perspective and understanding of the significance of the land/Earth than their white colonizers/oppressors. This difference makes it a dubious proposition for ecotheologians today to falsely universalize the sin of ecological devastation as a problem of the human species that "we" must solve together. Ecotheologians' admission that we live in an interconnected and interdependent universe and their call to move away

from classical notions of God as a king—who is disconnected
and removed from the concerns of his inferiors in his kingdom,
in favor of a God-symbol that reveals the interrelationship of all
creation on the Earth—is an essential and vitally necessary shift
in contemporary theology. Yet it is a shift that fails to account
for or acknowledge the history of repression of indigenous people and the subjugation of their voices and theological knowledge that expressed a similar view of the universe and existence.
"Whose Earth is it?" The inattention to this question manifests
the whiteness of ecotheology. Ecotheologians' attempt to solve
the problem reveals a blindness and a failure to face the truth
that ecological recovery is not a concern independent from the
struggle for racial justice and against European colonialism and
neocolonialism, because both are part and parcel of the same
problem—the problem of whiteness, specifically white epistemological hubris. I maintain a call for a theology of Pan-African
spatial recovery and renewal, or an Africana ecotheology, that
can begin to create a path toward reconciliation with the land
and the Earth. Such reconciliation calls for the promotion of
sacred memory, the overcoming of historical racial amnesia, and
the development of rituals of healing and renewal based on a
spatial orientation that gives attention to the legacy of blood-
soaked and resource-depleted spaces of Earth.

The essence of white epistemological hubris is the arrogant
assumption that the white/Western view of reality is objectively accurate and thus superior in the representation of the
universe relative to non-Western perspectives. It is a view centered on the individual, a view that deems technological innovation and the linear march toward scientific advancement and
technological and economic development to be implicitly correct, inevitable, and "progressive." This trek toward a type of
utopia, which derives from a theological longing to recreate the

Garden of Eden, is rarely questioned but is assumed to be the best approach, even what God would want. It is an extremely anthropocentric view of reality that assumes what is best for (white) human beings is what is best for the Earth and all who live therein.

This worldview prioritizes privatization, commodification, and individualism and has given rise to capitalism and neoliberalism. Non-white people, non-human creatures, and the lands on which they reside are reduced to mere cogs in the white techno-machine culture of progress. Specifically, the land has been victimized through mechanization, despiritualization, and objectification. The objectification and despiritualization of places of Earth is a function of the violence enshrined in the land as a consequence of the history of conquest. The land/Earth, like the non-white people who lived on it, was objectified and exploited for its natural resources and its ability to help the machine churn via the generation of capital and the creation of commodities. What was lacking is any acknowledgment that the land is a "living being" that precedes and determines human existence and is also an extension of human energy and vitality. Earth is not simply a cold, dead object created to serve human needs, wants, and greed.

White epistemological hubris as it relates to the Earth is crystallized in the philosophical underpinnings of the Europeanized concept of *private property*. Private property promotes both individualism and the objectification of the Earth. It is based on the notion that an individual can, or has a right to, possess a thing. It reduces the Earth, or carved-up sections of the Earth, to just another object over which one can have dominion. The idea of private property gained legitimacy in Roman common law and later was affirmed in English law. John Locke, English philosopher and Enlightenment thinker, offered a justification for private property stemming from glorification of the individual and their personal labor. He saw private property as a reward for human industrious labor:

> Though the Earth, and all inferior creatures be common to all Men, yet every Man has a property to his own person. This nobody has a right to but himself. The Labor of his body and the work of his Hands, we may say is properly his. Whatsoever then he removes out of state that nature hath provided, and left it in, he hath mixed his Labour with, and joined to it something that is his own, and thereby makes it his property.[1]

For Locke, then, the idea of private property emerges from a notion of individual merit in the context of a European Enlightenment critique of the church and hierarchical social systems and structures that breed dependency and resist individual critical reasoning and personal autonomy and agency. Land/Earth as private property is the consequence of fetishizing the individual man, the European man, in the midst of efforts to exalt his individual liberty. Locke's justification was never used, however, in furtherance of the rights of Native Americans. The indigenous people were only extensions of the wild Earth that needed taming by the industrious labor of white men.

Today globalization, or international Western capitalism, assumes the universal legitimacy of private property (justified through legal manipulation), never considering either the ramifications of what such a concept has wrought on the destruction of the land or the legacy of spatial dislocation and containment of marginalized and exploited Black bodies. Private property as

---

1. John Locke, *Two Treatises Concerning Government* (1690), chapter V, §27.

a legal concept helps manifest white epistemological hubris. It is also integral to the formation of free-market capitalism. The inequality generated by capitalism correlates with how the land, the Earth, is controlled by an elite few. If the land is owned by so few, how are we all equally responsible for its healing and recovery? How can the Earth heal if privatization of the Earth and its resources continues? How do we heal the Earth without attending to how whiteness and the Western Christian worldview spawned this devolution toward ecological disaster? Perhaps Christian theology, as a Western discipline, is limited in its ability to address these issues precisely because of its fixation with universalizing the reality of all human beings as equal victims of ontological sin. Such false universalization, a feature of white epistemological hubris, actually obfuscates the problem and impedes our ability to connect the issue of impending ecological devastation to the ideology of white supremacy.

A theological analysis is necessary because Western Christianity is thoroughly implicated in the worldview that evinces the problem, especially as represented in the Christian Doctrine of Discovery of 1493. The Catholic Church used this doctrine as the basis for conquest and "discovery" of non-European lands. The doctrine stated that land uninhabited by Christians was wild, untamed, and essentially available for domination, possession, and ownership. The land was untamed because it was inhabited by people who were untamed. Conquest of the land was a religious principle that extended from Christian evangelism and an appropriation of the exodus narrative in the Bible. The commodification of the land derives from the commodification of the people. This perspective views the natural world as objects to be possessed, controlled, and subdued.

However, traditional African spirituality sees the Earth differently. The traditional African worldview views the Earth, the land, as the predecessor and extension of all human and non-human beings who inhabit it. The Earth grants life and nurtures human beings. We are all dependent on it and subject to its rules and whims. An African-centered view of the Earth rejects the dominant biblical view grounded in a dominion paradigm. In Genesis 1:28, God declares to humankind, "Fill the Earth and subdue it. Have dominion over the fish of the sea and the birds of the air and over every living thing that moves on the Earth." This text helps establish human dominance over the rest of the natural world, as it convinced Christian readers that humans should dominate the Earth to conform it to human will. However, traditional African and Native American spiritualities reject the idea that we have dominion over the Earth or even that we are stewards of it; rather, our purpose is to maintain the balance and harmony that existed here before we arrived, and to be in right relation with the vital energy that we are composed of as human beings.

As such, "African morality cannot sanction the private ownership of land."[2] Human beings cannot monopolize the land and its resources for their own selfish purposes. Such monopolization (really by just a few and not by the masses) rejects the principle of reciprocity, failing to see the land as an equal. African and Native American spirituality both grant that what is taken from the Earth must be restored to the Earth. Rituals of animal sacrifice, offerings, and even ritual ceremonies like the Sun Dance that offer human flesh as an atonement are all forms of acknowledgment of the need for human beings to give back to the Earth in reciprocation for the things they have taken from the Earth.[3] Additionally, the African worldview has always

2. Laurenti Magesa, *African Religion: The Moral Traditions of Abundant Life* (Maryknoll, NY: Orbis Books, 1997), 63.
3. Tink Tinker, "American Indian Religious Traditions," in *The Hope of*

acknowledged what science has relatively recently discovered: that energy is neither created nor destroyed and that matter is just a particular configuration of energy. Human beings and the land/Earth we inhabit are energy beings. Thus, death is not really an end but a moment of transition to another energy configuration. The African worldview understands that, at death, energy (characterized as energy/spirit) returns to the land, or the natural world; consequently, "inanimate" natural objects possess and/or merge with the vital energies that were once human beings. Far from being inanimate, these natural entities are alive and continue to reflect some level of the sentience of the former human being. Africans recognize this presence as both ancestral spirits and nature spirits. All these entities exist in the same spatiotemporal reality; thus, from an African-centered point of view, nature has a spiritual potency and is a living reality, in stark contradiction to its objectification. As a result, nature cannot be possessed in the same way one might possess an object commonly found in Western culture, like a cellphone, a car, a house, or a laptop computer.

The differences in the traditional African and traditional Western Christian perceptions of the natural world are in part due to how each views human death and the *afterlife*. The traditional Western Christian view is derived from the Neoplatonic tradition of a stark dualistic reality with two distinct realms—the material world and the spiritual world. Kelly Brown Douglas describes it as the Platonized tradition within Western Christianity.[4] The natural world is part of the material, a world that is decaying, the realm of sin. Nature is part of the sinful realm of

Liberation in World Religions, ed. Miguel A. De La Torre (Waco, TX: Baylor University Press, 2008), 265.

4. Kelly Brown Douglas, *What's Faith Got to Do with It? Black Bodies/Christian Souls* (Maryknoll, NY: Orbis Books, 2005).

humankind confined by spatiotemporal limitations. It is earth-bound. Only the spiritual realm is the realm of God and the place where redeemed souls will spend eternity. Douglas argues that the apostle Paul and St. Augustine of Hippo are the chief, and most influential, proponents of this Platonized Christian theology. Augustine, in particular, subjugated the body in favor of the rationality of the soul. His ideas would later be appropriated by white evangelical Christians in a way that led to the subjugation, even demonization, of Black bodies, who, like Native Americans, were equated with and considered aspects of the natural (sinful) world.

But the traditional African perspective recognizes only one spatiotemporal reality, and the ancestors and other spiritual entities that reside in the same spatiotemporal reality constitute the link between the visible and invisible entities. The natural world is that link because ancestral spirits maintain existence there and use bodies of water as vehicles to transition from the visible realm to the realm of the ancestors. In this sense, unlike Platonized Christianity, the traditional African worldview is an earthbound theology, which makes it a suitable conversation partner for Christian ecotheology. Josiah Young states it succinctly: "The traditional African … is stubbornly earthbound, determined in many cases to return to the earth in someone or something. For the most part, the African does not hope for eternal life in the 'good heaven.'"[5] The African understanding of the ancestor, then, is the linchpin that has implications for the view of nature. The land is revered because it is the place where one's ancestors lived while in the visible plane, and it continues to be the place that manifests the vital energy and spiritual

5. Josiah Young, "Out of Africa: Traditional African Religion and African Theology," in *World Religions and Human Liberation*, ed. Dan Cohn-Sherbok (Maryknoll, NY: Orbis Books, 1992), 100.

presence of the deceased. Thus, the land connects generations. According to Vincent Mulago,

> The living, for their part, must go on receiving the vital inflow from the ancestors and departed relatives, or their life will wither. Strength, life is the first thing asked for in all prayers addressed to the ancestors, the departed parents, to the spirits of protecting heroes, and in the wishes in which the Supreme Being is mentioned and asked to intervene.[6]

The natural world is the connective tissue that binds the visible with the invisible through the ancestor symbol. Spatial dislocation, rupture, and confinement through land dispossession then inevitably lead to spiritual and cultural alienation and fragmentation. This chapter will examine the legacy of this land dispossession and the resulting spiritual alienation and ecological devastation.

Josiah Young provides a good synopsis of the African understanding of the Earth. In arguing that liberation theologies have something to learn from African traditional religion, he concludes,

> African traditional religion can also sensitize liberation theologians to the necessity to respect the "livingness" of the environment. Indeed the ancestors remind us that the earth is our home, and the prolongation of humankind is intimately bound to the Earth's fecundity. The sky, the earth, and all the living and breathing things that give life and balance to the cosmos are essential in the quest for a new humanity (Fanon). And so the

---

6. Magesa, *African Religion,* 147.

ancestors teach us that we must listen to this earth, feel
its pulse, if we are to recognize our connection to the
sacred. African traditional religion reminds liberation
theologians of the sacredness of the invisible—the reality of the sacred and the involvement of divinity in all
that pertains to health and wholeness.[7]

The African View of Nature and Space in the New World

This traditional African view of the Earth and perception of
nature did not remain solely within the geographical terrain of
the continent, and it is vital to note that it traveled across the
Atlantic with the human beings held captive in slave ships. They
took Africa with them. Enslaved Africans' view of the natural
world differed immensely from that of white enslavers and colonizers. This would have serious implications, especially after
slavery, when African-descended people painstakingly acquired
land in America only to have much of it stolen from them—in
many instances after they were killed in acts of racist violence
exacerbated by capitalist greed and consumption.

First, however, I examine Charles Long's reframing of religious experience in light of African people's dispossession from
the land mass Africa. He defines religion as "an orientation in
the ultimate sense ... how one comes to terms with the ultimate
significance of one's life."[8] Long then notes the implications
of this definition. "First of all it implies a geographical sense
of things and like all geographies it has to do with the location of various forms of materiality in space. Part of knowing

7. Young, "Out of Africa," 107.

8. Charles H. Long, *The Collected Writings of Charles H. Long: Ellipsis*
(New York: Bloomsbury, 2018), 253.

who one is means coming to know where one is located. This is true for people as well as individuals."[9] The spatial dislocation of dark bodies from Africa caused a disorientation and reorientation in the "New" World. Black religion in the Western world, according to Long, struggles thereafter to be reconciled with this diasporic reality. This wrestling constitutes the basic substrata of Black religion: "the image and historical reality of Africa; the involuntary presence of African-Americans in the United States; and the experience of God in the religious experiences of blacks."[10]

The involuntary presence of Black people in America, Long argues, happens in concert with the genocide of the aboriginal people and the theft of their land. African diasporic peoples' reconstructed spirituality is derivative of their spatial disorientation and sense of geographical alienation as subjects in a religiously oppressive state of captivity. Given this, I contend that it is a vital necessity to examine certain African rituals brought over to America through a spatial prioritization, by examining the attempt to reorient the new space in the context of cultural contact and exchange with Protestant Christian Europeans. The ring shout is one such ritual that captures the essence not only of religio-cultural contact with Europeans (who would become white) but also of displaced Africans' need for vital spatial recovery and reconnection.

The ring shout is an African ritual that helped convert displaced Africans to Protestant forms of Christianity while simultaneously Africanizing the space and the land they were forced to inhabit. Sterling Stuckey makes clear that the ring shout is a West African ritual brought to America to assist in reori-

9. Long, *Collected Writings*, 253.
10. Charles H. Long, *Significations: Signs, Symbols, and Images in the Interpretation of Religion* (Aurora, CO: The Davies Group, 1999), 188.

enting enslaved Africans into a white Christian environment. Long agrees with Stuckey that, through the ritual of the ring shout, Black people Africanized, or indigenized, the new spaces they were forced to inhabit in North America. He asserts, "The ring shout dance, a movement remembered by the body from Africa, became the initiatory rhythm that brought new Africans into the moral community created by the enslaved Africans in America. Thus, in this one rhythmic movement of the body, the newly enslaved Africans recreated Africa in the same moment that they became American."[11]

Assimilated Black Christian minister Rev. Daniel Payne, in his memoirs, maligned the ring shout as just another African heathen practice he hoped to abolish. However, his mere reference to it in the early postbellum period (the 1890s) demonstrates the persistence not just of Africanisms in Black spirituality in America but of concerted efforts by Black people to recreate Africa in America, to achieve Pan-African spatial recovery, reconnection, and healing. When Payne interviewed the pastor to whom he discouraged the practice, the pastor contended, "There must be a ring here, a ring there, a ring over yonder, or sinners will not get converted."[12] In other words, Black people's conversion to Protestant Christianity required that they bridge the space, the gulf between America and Africa. Conversion necessitated sanctification of the new land, in order to Africanize America. Then "sinners could be converted" to accept Jesus. Ironically, the process of religio-cultural assimilation of Black people to an American Protestant Christian worldview required a symbolic, geographical, spatial conversion of North America to West Africa.

11. Charles H. Long, "Bodies in Time and The Healing of Spaces," in *Collected Writings*, 268.

12. Daniel Alexander Payne, *Recollections of Seventy Years* (first published, 1888; repr., New York: Arno Press, 1968), 253–55.

Payne emphasized the repugnance he felt toward Blacks who participated in ring shouts, and he wrote that he had encountered them "in many places." Among those most amenable to Anglo-Saxon Christian assimilation, he was able to discourage the practice. However, among the "ignorant masses … it was regarded as the essence of religion."[13] This is one of many examples of displaced Africans, now formerly enslaved, filtering and discerning Christianity through an African-centered lens. We also see how the more assimilated and Western-educated, Black religious authorities among them evinced anti-Black, anti-African Christian sentiment. Yet the ring shout was essential to making Christianity acceptable to the majority of Black converts at the time. What Black Christian theologians have not analyzed about the history of the ring shout is what such a ritual practice meant for how these displaced Africans viewed the space, the land they consecrated by way of the ring shout. They have not examined the ring shout as an exercise of conjuration.

Jason Young, however, describes the ring shout and enslaved Africans' religious experiences in praise houses in the antebellum South as acts of resistance, improvisation, and free will. The praise houses, where the ring shout and communal experiences of spirit possession and ecstatic worship occurred, was Africanized space set apart. "In dancing the ring shout, with its slow, sedimented steps inscribed around an ever-revolving circle, slaves marked off an autonomous sphere of spiritual practice. Taken together, praise-house worship … comprised an invaluable space over which slaves maintained ultimate control."[14] Young notes that white overseers and planters eventually became suspi-

13. Payne, *Recollections of Seventy Years*, 253–55.
14. Jason R. Young, *Rituals of Resistance: African Atlantic Religion in Kongo and the Lowcountry South in the Era of Slavery* (Baton Rouge: Louisiana State University Press, 2007), 98.

cious of the religious autonomy and spiritual agency expressed
by the enslaved in these spaces. Nat Turner's slave insurrection
led to an almost complete cessation of worship in praise houses,
as white owners sought strict surveillance and oversight of the
Black religious experience. After 1831, the praise house was for-
bidden in favor of Blacks being forced to worship in the confined spaces of white church balconies and galleries. Such efforts
mark a type of additional spiritual and spatial dislocation and
rigid containment and surveillance that characterizes much of
the Black experience in America broadly.

The Africanization of America in spatial terms also has implications for the perception of the natural environment and the
new land on which these displaced Africans resided. The Gullah
people in the South Carolina Lowcountry epitomize attempts
to preserve West African traditions in the North American context. They believed that nature was teeming with spiritual power
and agency they often referred to as *simbi*. The simbi resist
explicit categorization in Western terms. Some have referred to
them as "lesser spirits" or "lesser deities." Some simbi are ancestral spirits, local spirits, or territorial spirits. They are markers of
sacred space, Africanized space, and they epitomize the spiritual
potency of nature. In the South Carolina Lowcountry, the simbi
represent a mechanism through which the people deal with a
host of spiritual issues. Ras Michael Brown states,

> This wide range of roles has allowed people to perceive
> and portray the simbi as nature spirits as well as local
> shrine spirits, ancestral spirits, non-lineal spirits of
> the dead, living people (especially children born with
> unusual characteristics and the extremely elderly), ani-
> mals, natural objects (most notably stones) and forms
> of energy. The simbi thus resist easy and exclusive cat-

egorization as beings in both the visible and invisible realms.[15]

The simbi represent the connection or link between the visible plane and the invisible spiritual realm, which are both a part of the natural world in the consciousness of the African mind. As such they offer insight into perceptions of the physical space, the land, and displaced Africans' understanding that the land constitutes sacred space that must be respected and viewed as mysterious and awe-inspiring.

> The simbi have usually occupied features of the natural environment, particularly pools (of springs and waterfalls), rivers, streams, rocks, stones, forests and mountains. It was in these locations that people encountered the simbi, whether the living sought out the simbi intentionally or stumbled upon them accidentally. But like the shrine-based spirits of West-Central Africa, the simbi also affected the weather and the condition of the flora and fauna … controlling the natural environment.[16]

Because the simbi reside in the natural environment, they represent not only the idea that nature is alive and conscious but also that it is literally an extension of human beings. The simbi conjoin the African notion of ancestors with other *forms of energy* that have the power to determine climatic outcomes and the utility of the plants and herbs in the surrounding areas. As such they reveal the traditional West African understanding

---

15. Ras Michael Brown, *African-Atlantic Cultures and the South Carolina Lowcountry* (Cambridge: Cambridge University Press, 2012), 31.

16. Brown, *African-Atlantic Cultures*, 29.

that human beings do not possess some superior relationship to the Earth permitting them to express dominance and ownership, but that the natural world is, in part, an extension of human energies, visible and invisible, reconfigured into flora, fauna, and bodies of water. Thus, cutting down trees or drilling into the Earth for oil or other resources for mere commercial gain is anathema to West African ancestral values and their view of the land as sacred. It constitutes a violent spiritual breach that stands in stark opposition to African religio-cultural values.

I discuss the ring shout ritual, praise houses, and the simbi as a part of the early religious experiences of African Americans to make the point that West Africans who were held captive, stolen, and displaced to America brought Africa with them and then conjured American spaces as African, despite efforts by whites and by those Blacks who internalized whiteness, to stamp out or prevent this. They sacralized, honored, and indigenized/ Africanized the natural spaces around them. Their perception of that natural space is crucial when we consider our current ecological decline in concert with the long legacy of vicious land dispossession in this "New World" and in colonial and postcolonial Africa.

THE LEGACY OF STOLEN EARTH IN AMERICA

The precious lands that Black people acquired during and after slavery in America were often stolen from them in the twentieth century, both through brutal violence, especially during the period of lynching in America, and also through manipulation of American legal procedures that made sacred the concept of private property and tied it to a racist conceptualization of citizenship. Much of this history has been forgotten or sanitized, a part of the historical, racial amnesia or deliberate misremembering that constitutes too much of the experience of both Black and white people in the twenty-first century. I unearth the history as part of a larger conversation about the ecological crisis that confronts all human beings on planet Earth. Whose worldviews, whose cultures, and whose philosophical and theological perceptions of land/Earth were allowed to manifest, not just in America but throughout the world, and thus are most responsible for our current planetary realities? Conversely, whose worldviews and theology of land were repressed and constitute subjugated knowledge, the consequences of which have had a devastating impact on the natural world?

While it would be problematic to view this in overly simplistic binary terms since cultural contact and exchange are inevitable, it is crucial to note that not all humans have shared the same view of Earth and how to inhabit it. This is important, because the pathway to ecological recovery and restoration is not a single, linear path through Western technological innovation and cultural normativity. I ask the previous questions not merely to assign blame and deflect responsibility for climate change but to highlight the white epistemological hubris implicated here and name and reject its continued hidden presence in the policy initiatives of Western governments and even in ecological justice movements around the world. There is a reckoning that must take place first—an accounting of the perspectives rendered primitive and heathen, the lives lost, and the lands stolen in blood-soaked earth where violence is enshrined. Rituals of sacred memory must be performed in order to re-sacralize the land and heal the Earth.

The vast majority of Black land dispossessions occurred in Southern states in America throughout the twentieth century. "In 1910, black Americans owned at least 15 million acres of farmland, nearly all of it in the south, according to the U.S. Agricultural Census. Today blacks own only 1.1 million acres of farmland and are part owners of another 1.07 million."[17] While the number of white farmers also has declined, as corporate farming concentrates large swaths of farmland into the hands of fewer individuals, "black ownership has declined at 2½ times faster than white ownership according to a 1982 federal report."[18] So many of the stories of vicious Black land dispossession are tied to incidents of white racist violence and intimidation in Southern states. The Associate Press discovered and reported fifty-seven violent land takings in an eighteen-month investigation of Black land loss in America. "If you're looking for stolen black land, just follow the lynching trail."[19] I note just a few such instances in the paragraphs below.

> After midnight on Oct. 4 1908, 50 hooded white men surrounded the home of a black farmer in Hickman, Ky., and ordered him to come out for a whipping. When David Walker refused and shot at them instead, the mob set fire to his house.… Walker ran out, followed by four screaming children and his wife with a baby in her arm. The mob shot them all, wounding three children and killing the others. Walker's oldest son never made it out the burning house. No one was ever charged in the killings, and the surviving children were deprived of the land their father died to defend. Records show that Walker's 2½ acre farm was simply folded into the property of a white neighbor.[20]

17. Todd Lewan and Dolores Barclay, "When They Steal Your Land, They Steal Your Future," *Los Angeles Times*, December 2, 2001.

18. Barclay, "When They Steal Your Land."

19. Thad Sitton and James H. Conrad, *Freedom Colonies: Independent Black Texans in the Time of Jim Crow* (Austin: University of Texas Press, 2005), 178.

20. Sitton and Conrad, *Freedom Colonies*, 178.

This is merely one example of a pattern of white racist violence and tax and land law manipulation that constitutes the history of White America's unacknowledged license to engage in racist land theft from African Americans. Another example is the story of Rev. Isaac Simmons of Amite County, Mississippi.

> In 1942, his 141-acre farm was sold for nonpayment of taxes, property records show. The farm, for which his father paid $302 in 1887, was bought by a white man for $180. Only partial, tattered records for the period exist today in the county courthouse, but they are enough to show that tax payments on at least one of the property were current when the land was taken. Simmons hired a lawyer in February 1944 and filed a suit to regain his land. On March 26, a group of whites paid Simmons a visit … the men [dragged Simmons away].… The whites then grabbed Simmons' son, Eldridge, from his house and drove the two men to a lonely road. "Two of them kept beating me.… They kept telling me my father and I were [acting too smart] for going to see a lawyer.…" Later that day the minister's body turned up with three gunshot wounds in the back, the McComb Enterprise newspaper reported at the time.[21]

These instances of racist brutality exemplify not only the sinful defilement and destruction of Black bodies but also the dispossession and defilement of portions of the Earth. These vicious land grabs are examples of the mantra "might makes right" and demonstrate the truth that Black people had no legal recourse or any avenue of protection against white racist brutality. Black people often died defending and preserving their land,

---

21. Sitton and Conrad, *Freedom Colonies*, 178.

and the blood-soaked earth still cries out for reconciliation and restitution. The destruction and defilement of their bodies correlate to the subjugation and dismissal of their African-derived perspectives on, and intentions for, the land.

In Mississippi, William F. Holmes notes, "Whitecapping specifically meant the attempt to force a person to abandon his home or property; it meant driving Negroes off land they owned or rented."[22] Such land theft often reinforced blackness as inferior.

> Eli Hilson was murdered because he did not limit his aspirations to laboring for whites, and this independence was unacceptable. Possibly even more significant than Eli Hilson himself was the fear that other Lincoln Country blacks might see him as a role model and follow in his footsteps, acquiring land, banking assets, and trying to break away from white domination. Former Mississippi governor James K. Vardaman proclaimed, "If it is necessary every Negro in the state will be lynched; it will be done to maintain white supremacy."[23]

Then there is the example of Forsyth County, Georgia, in 1912, which can only be described as a racial purging or cleansing: over one thousand black residents were either killed or run out of town by white mobs posing as vigilantes. In September 1912, three Black male field workers were accused of raping a white woman. All were eventually lynched and shot when local white mobs stormed the jails and captured the accused, preempting due process and a trial by jury. Waves of *night riders* burned the property of, terrorized, and ran out all 1,098 Black

22. William Holmes, "Whitecapping: Agrarian Violence in Mississippi, 1902–1906," *Journal of Southern History* 35.2 (May 1969): 166.

23. Stewart E. Tolnay and E. M. Beck, *A Festival of Violence: An Analysis of Southern Lynchings 1882–1930* (Urbana: University of Illinois Press, 1995), 25.

residents from the county. These night rides were motivated by white fear that presumed the Black people in the county were angry and planning a violent racial response to the unjust lynching of the accused Black men. Of course there is no evidence that "Black riots" were being planned, but the expectation of a Black backlash laid the foundation and rationale for a vicious, violent racial purging by the white residents. The purging included looting the livestock and eventually inconspicuously assuming ownership of the "abandoned" properties, which included many Black farms and Black church property. Forsyth County would remain all white well into the 1990s.[24] Journalist Elliot Jaspin notes that the vast majority of the Black residents in Forsyth either sold their properties at artificially low prices or were made to simply walk away, knowing their white neighbors would eventually assume ownership.

For thirty-four of the black landowners, there is no record that they ever sold their land. It made no difference. Whites, money in hand, would pay the tax on the land they did not own and the clerk would note the transaction … simply ignoring the gap in ownership.… In the three years after the expulsion, nearly two-thirds of the black-owned farmland that had not been sold was appropriated in this way.[25]

While reports of the extent of this racial cleansing are sparse, the *Augusta Chronicle* reported at the time that "a score or more of homes have been burned during the past few weeks … and five Negro churches."[26]

The burning of Black churches is especially poignant as a mechanism of expulsion due to the church's role in Black com-

24. Patrick Phillips, *Blood at the Root: A Racial Cleansing in America* (New York: W.W. Norton, 2016), 184.
25. Elliot Jaspin, *Buried in the Bitter Waters: The Hidden History of Racial Cleansing in America* (New York: Basic Books, 2007), 136.
26. "Forsyth People Ask for Troops," *Augusta Chronicle,* October 19, 1912.

munities at this time. The church was an institution that tended to the total person; it provided not only spiritual encouragement but also political, social, educational, and occupational enrichment. According to W. E. B. Du Bois, the Black church was "the most characteristic expression of African character."[27] In *Souls of Black Folk,* he explains that the Black church

> is the central club-house of the community of Negroes. Various institutions meet here—the church proper, the Sunday-school, two or three insurance societies, women's societies, secret societies, and mass meetings of various kinds. Entertainments, suppers, and lectures are held.… Considerable sums of money are collected and expended here, employment is found for the idle, strangers are introduced, news is disseminated and charity distributed.[28]

Thus, the destruction of a Black church was more than the demolishment of a building but constituted the destruction of the hub and nexus of Black existence in predominantly white spaces. The church was the essence of Black self-determination in most areas in the South because it was the only independent institution owned and controlled by Black people. Destruction of the buildings constituted further spatial dislocation, alienation, and purging.

A Second Spatial Dislocation

The Forsyth County example serves as a microcosm of the brutal racial violence and land theft inflicted upon Black people

---

27. W. E. B. Du Bois, *The Souls of Black Folk* (Chicago: A. C. McClurg, 1903), 136.
   28. Du Bois, *Souls of Black Folk*, 136.

and original indigenous people throughout the world, not just in North America but elsewhere, including on the continent of Africa. White imperialists still continue using violence and/or Western legal maneuvering to take land that is not theirs and then exploit that land for its natural resources to profit and fuel their economies. Vicious land grabs are essentially violent acts of domination that make a mockery of the cultural values of those despoiled and vanquished. According to African spirituality, however, the Earth does not forget even though new generations of humans do. The land absorbs the blood, the deaths, and the unreconciled loss. The Forsyth County example is instructive, because it serves as just one example of the incalculable loss, not just of land but of Black agency, ingenuity, and power. Lynching was a mechanism of terror and social control that whites instituted "when they felt threatened in some way—economically, politically, or socially."[29] Lynching, and the accompanying land theft, reveal the vapidity of whiteness—the extent to which its core feature is insecurity, incompleteness, and an insatiable quest for an unattainable wholeness. As human bodies were abused and exploited, so too was the land. In spatial terms, Black people in America were dislocated and dispossessed twice, being made to suffer the initial journey across the Atlantic in chains and then a second dispossession from lands in the South to more compact, confined urban areas in the North and West. White America's reneging on the promise of forty acres and a mule is connected to ecological decay and disturbance as well as racial terror.

Long insists that African-descended peoples' acceptance of Western modes of time and space constitute an overlooked mechanism of control and a feature of oppression. He calls encounters between Europeans and non-Europeans *contact*

---

29. Tolnay and Beck, *Festival of Violence*, 3.

zones, where the dominated eventually internalize the Christian notion of time and history. He asserts,

> When Europeans made contact with non-European cultures in various parts of the world, they were armed with ideological cultural notions not simply regarding what was normative for them but, in addition, their norms were understood to be normative for all human-kind. While they were more often than not bearers of superior military, navigational, and other forms of tech-nology, it was their normative understanding of time and space that they desired to force upon those whom they met.[30]

What Long describes is what I name as *white epistemologi-cal hubris*. It is the assumption that what is true and the norm for whites is true and should be the norm for all humankind. Long contends that Black people's acceptance of Western modes of time and space is as devastating as the massive land loss. Through acts of spatial terror, conquest, and conversion to Western Christian modes of understanding, Black people in America adjusted their lives and, in an effort to survive, con-formed to confinement on a far more limited spatial terrain. Similar to the conditions during American chattel slavery, when enslaved Africans were forced out of their own praise houses and into balconies where they could be confined and more closely surveilled by whites, this postbellum land dispossession forced a larger and more devastating process of spatial containment that prevented Africanizing or indigenizing these spaces in North America, these sections of Earth. Additionally, many Black people bought into the seductive myth of racial and economic

30. Long, "Transculturation and Religion," in *Significations*, 149.

progress, which decentered prioritization and spiritualization of the land and placed emphasis on the individual worker, who was encouraged to work hard and use time efficiently and effectively.

Adjustment to a Christian capitalistic orientation that configures the human being primarily as worker and laborer posited the North and West as places of economic opportunity during a period of rapid industrialization. These places, however, forced confinement in smaller, compact urban dwellings, increasing alienation from the natural world (the land) that was, in part, the holder and preserver of African religio-cultural values. The ancestors are tied to the land both in Africa and in the Southern states of America, and the Great Migration was a process in furtherance of spatial alienation from the land/Earth, yet it is often interpreted as racial economic progress.

The experience of Black people in Chicago, Illinois, provides one example. Immigrant whites in Chicago accepted and promulgated many of the same racist tropes toward Blacks that fueled the white lynch-mob mentality in the South, such as hypersexual deviancy and interracial interaction (specifically regarding Black men with white women). In places like Chicago, however, these myths were used to fortify the police force and begin the process of connecting policing with strict surveillance and rigid spatial containment and control of Black bodies. "In Chicago, modern policing emerged as a system of control to respond to interracial socializing and sex."[31] Racist texts like Frederick L. Hoffman's *Race Traits*[32] warned whites of the Black people migrating to the North, fleeing racial terror in

31. Rashad Shabazz, *Spatializing Blackness: Architectures of Confinement and Black Masculinity in Chicago* (Urbana: University of Illinois Press, 2015), 30.

32. Frederick L. Hoffman, *Race Traits and Tendencies of the American Negro* (New York: American Economic Association by the Macmillan Company, 1896).

the South. Fears of Chicago becoming too African prompted a geographical configuration in which whites essentially reimplemented Jim Crow segregation without the "Whites Only" signs. According to Hoffman, white people should "seal themselves off from" Black people in order to ensure their own survival and protection.[33]

Policing was, and continues to be, framed in the context of protecting a vulnerable white population from the wanton criminality and sexual deviancy of Black people. Redlining specific Black areas of the city, coupled with overpolicing, generated a Black geography marked by rigid spatial containment in the midst of economic blight in housing projects. This forced masses of Black people into cramped, overcrowded living conditions in smaller spaces, increasing their alienation from the land and the Earth, once a source of spiritual agency, culture, and connection. Michelle Alexander is right that carceral power did become a New Jim Crow, especially in the North. Moreover, even worse than in the South, there was an even greater reality of spatial limitation and confinement both in and outside of prison.[34] In other words, carceral spaces extend beyond mass incarceration and actually include the confined spatial terrain in which Blacks are forced to exist outside of prison.

The false narrative of racial progress in America continues, however, despite the tremendous spatial regression and loss Black people have experienced since slavery. The myth of racial progress relies on acceptance of the preeminence of time over space in Western values and modalities. The idea that Black people in America have incrementally improved their situation views racial contact through the lens of Western linear thought

33. Shabazz, *Spatializing Blackness*, 25.

34. Michelle Alexander, *The New Jim Crow: Mass Incarceration in the Age of Colorblindness* (New York: The New Press, 2010).

and ignores the truth that racist ideas have evolved along with racist liberal efforts at racial amelioration. Ibram X. Kendi is explicit about this in his work: "In order to fully explain the complex history of racist ideas, *Stamped from the Beginning* must chronicle this racial progress and the simultaneous progression of racist policies. Hate and ignorance have not driven the history of racist ideas in America. Racist policies have driven the history of racist ideas in America."[35] The myth of racial progress underscores the rejection of an African-centered spatial orientation and actually functions only to assuage white guilt.

In spatial terms, Black people currently own and reside on less land and have access to and control over fewer natural resources than they had one hundred years ago. Any discussion of the government granting reparations for the long history of American racial suffering and subjugation would be less than a half-measure if it does not include the recovery and restoration of land and an honest reckoning with the long legacy of Black land dispossession. However, my theological proposal focuses on Black self-determination and calls upon Black churches particularly, but also other Black religious institutions, to reject spatial confinement and reclaim and restore the Earth by acquiring land and greening/healing, or indigenizing, those spaces. I am calling for Black churches to develop a Pan-African theology of spatial recovery and restoration as Earth-bound human beings in order to honor the legacy of lost spaces but also as a practical effort to heal and restore the Earth, our only home. This includes creating and cultivating rituals of remembrance that honor those blood-soaked places of Earth where Black self-determination was murdered.

---

35. Ibram X. Kendi, *Stamped from the Beginning: The Definitive History of Racist Ideas in America* (New York: Hachette Book Group, 2017), 9.

Native Land Dispossession in Africa

The numerous examples of Black land dispossession in America are dwarfed by the legacy of land theft that also occurred in Africa and is similarly the result of the vicious legacy of white supremacy. Recall Long's first point regarding the substratum of how Black religion in America is the image and religious symbol of Africa. My examination of land loss and the impact of Western modes of time as a modality of disorientation for African and African-descended peoples requires discussion of the impacts of European colonization and imperialism and the depletion of natural resources on the continent of Africa. While the history of European colonization is extensive, with virtually all of the massive continent of Africa being colonized, I will focus on two examples from West and southern Africa. These examples function as paradigmatic symbols of spatial-terrain abuse and dislocation in furtherance of European/Western authority's pursuit of power through the accumulation of resources and capital.

West Africa, particularly the nation of Ghana, historically suffered from traditional colonialism that led to the indigenous people fighting for and declaring their independence from the British metropole. Ghana is an important example for this analysis and discussion, as it was the first African nation to declare its independence (1957) from a European nation. Kwame Nkrumah was the first president of the new, supposedly "sovereign" nation. More than sixty years after independence, however, Ghana still does not fully control its own land and natural resources. Nkrumah's concept of "neocolonialism," which will be discussed shortly, is a critique of Western recommendations for African development. His analysis led to a plan to create spatial reconciliation and recovery as well as his vision for African socialism and an initial proposal to create a United States of Africa. While Ghana represents a relatively small segment of physical land/Earth, it symbolizes the effects of traditional colonialism in West and West Central Africa. The nefarious undermining and subverting of Nkrumah's presidency by the United States, specifically the Central Intelligence Agency's role in supporting the coup that toppled Nkrumah's administration, represents a loss for the Earth and the African social values his stated goals could have achieved for the continent writ large.[36]

South Africa is a different example of settler colonialism because the colonizers from both Belgium and England settled in the land after 1652. The indigenous people suffered the indignities of war over land and then apartheid, which is principally about land dispossession and spatial containment of the natives on so-called homelands. In the aftermath of the official end of legalized apartheid in 1994 and the implementation of the new charter, South Africa still has not resolved its racist history of land theft and displacement. Political liberation (the African National Congress is now the most influential political party in South Africa) has not addressed the persistent problem of land dispossession as the white minority continues to own and control the vast majority of land in South Africa and conforms to global capitalist initiatives. Both Ghana and South Africa are symbols of the legacy of European colonialism, a manifestation of whiteness and the different ways land displacement and abuse occur on the continent of Africa.

Exploitation of the land/Earth throughout postcolonial Africa can be explained by examining the effects of globalization on the land in Africa, specifically the impact of global corporate industrial agribusiness, a subset of neocolonialism and neoliberalism. Neoliberalism is a byproduct of white epistemological hubris and places primacy on individualism and profit

---

36. John Stockwell, *In Search of Enemies: A CIA Story* (New York: W. W. Norton, 1978), 201n.

motive as the drivers of human will, reasoning, and behavior. Neoliberalism is what Keri Day calls "a rationality that structures and governs human conduct and behavior with societies that employ markets. Neoliberalism is a market rationale that orders people to live by the generalized principle of competition in *all* social spheres of life, making the individual herself or himself an enterprise."[37] She goes on to assert how a neoliberal moral framework informs individual choice, self-perception, and one's understanding of personal liberties, and she rejects the market principle that competition should be the "organizing principle of all human life."[38] Her framing of the category of neoliberalism is useful in connecting it with the current exploitation and abuse of land in Africa by global corporate agribusiness.

Corporate agribusiness is one example of how neocolonialism manifests itself in Africa. It essentially robs independent African nations, many formerly colonized by European nations, of their sovereignty and prevents national or local control of the land. Corporate industrial agribusiness, which also occurs in the United States, is the model of agriculture promoted by the World Bank and the World Trade Organization. It symbolizes the globalization of neocolonialism and its devastating effect on land/Earth. Contrary to myths associated with corporate agribusiness, this system both increases human hunger and further contributes to the destruction of the environment and the soil. "Industrial agriculture has greatly added to poverty by driving out local farmers and thus making more and more people dependent on buying high priced imported foods, rather than growing it locally themselves."[39] The idea that corporations can

---

37. Keri Day, *Religious Resistance to Neoliberalism: Womanist and Black Feminist Perspectives* (New York: Palgrave Macmillan, 2015), 8.

38. Day, *Religious Resistance to Neoliberalism*, 13.

39. Rosemary Radford Ruether, *Integrating Ecofeminism, Globalization, and World Religions* (Lanham, MD: Rowman & Littlefield, 2005), 15.

own the patent on a seed also disempowers local farming. Additionally, corporate agribusiness harms the soil and the environment through its heavy use of pesticides. These practices have had a particularly harmful impact on African nations because they have accelerated climate change and have simultaneously worked to thwart an alternative view of the land and a political economy generated from the land.

Ghana declared its independence from Great Britain in 1957 after having formerly been known in Western parlance as the Gold Coast. In reality, it is the home of various native ethnic groups, including the Akan, Ga, Ewe, Fante, and others, who embraced the more traditional African understanding of the land described earlier. The Europeanization of the geographical contours of the land continues to be a source of tension today as ethnic groups like the Asante, who have had a recognized kingdom for over one thousand years, are asked to conform to a sixty-five-year postcolonial identity predicated on European-established spatial parameters. In other words, national identity (Ghanaian) is sometimes at odds with ethnic identity (Asante). Too often this is framed through a Western lens as *tribalism*, simply because these African people would rather adhere to their traditional spatial configurations than to Western ones. *Tribalism* is a derisive term used to suggest that indigenous peoples are uncivilized, primitive, and prone to disunity or division. Tribalism in Africa is often a consequence of contestations deriving from efforts to prioritize a traditional African identity over a pseudo-European, or postcolonial one. The question of identity has implications for land usage and ownership and makes Nkrumah a relevant figure in assessing the difference in the current postcolonial reality and the potential for the land, in Ghana and throughout much of Africa.

President Nkrumah warned of impending neocolonialism in African nations masked as a postcolonial, independent sovereignty. His warning has implications for the exploitation of land and its natural resources, and how the language of "development" and the assumption of Western "free-market" superiority perpetuates ecological erosion, land dispossession, and poverty among the majority of Africa's citizens. Nkrumah defines *neo-colonialism* as a situation in which a former colony appears to be independent "and has all the outward trappings of international sovereignty. In reality, its economic system and thus its political policy is directed from outside."[40] In his work, *Consciencism*, he describes it this way:

> Neo-colonialism is a greater danger to independent countries than is colonialism. Colonialism is crude, essentially overt, and apt to be overcome by a purposeful concert of national effort. In neo-colonialism, however, the people are divided from their leaders and, instead of providing true leadership and guidance which is informed at every point by the ideal of the general welfare, leaders come to neglect the very people who put them in power and incautiously become instruments of suppression on behalf of the neo-colonialists.[41]

The problem of neocolonialism has ramifications for the exploitation of Africa's land and its resources but also for the African socialist perspective, which it thwarted, and the lost potential for a federation within a United States of Africa.

Again, not everyone shares or agrees with the Western capitalistic view of the land and how it should be used. Frantz Fanon agreed with Nkrumah that former colonial authorities would

---

40. Kwame Nkrumah, *Neo-colonialism: The Last Stage of Imperialism* (London: Panaf, 1974), 1.

41. Kwame Nkrumah, *Consciencism: Philosophy and Ideology for Decolonization* (New York: NYU Press, 1970), 102.

seek to maintain continual economic and political influence over their former colony.

> You may see colonialism withdrawing its capital and its technicians and setting up around the young state the apparatus of economic pressure. The apotheosis of independence is transformed into the curse of independence, and the colonial power through its immense resources of coercion condemns the young nation to regression. In plain words, the colonial power says "Since you want independence, take it and starve."[42]

African nations seeking to exercise true sovereignty would have to either incorporate austerity measures that would make independence feel worse than colonialism, or African leaders would be forced to choose the path of least resistance and cooperate with private foreign actors who would eventually control too much of the land and too many resources of the newly formed state.

One of the current manifestations of this neocolonialism is the way that foreign corporations engage in *land grabs*. Through land grabs, foreign companies gain access to numerous tracts of fertile land in African nations to conduct their agribusiness, often displacing the indigenous people who may be similarly using the land for local agricultural purposes. According to Mark Langan, "Foreign companies have negotiated land deals with African governments, which lead to the displacement of indigenous communities. Oftentimes, this is done in the name of 'development' and economic progress—with the implication that the indigenous villagers are backward and unproductive. This is despite the fact that subsistence agriculture in the tra-

---

42. Frantz Fanon, *The Wretched of the Earth*, trans. Constance Farrington (New York: Grove Press, 1963), 97.

ditional manner is the backbone of food security."[43] Langan claims that corporate land grabs for agribusiness and foreign companies' extraction of oil are contemporary manifestations of the neocolonialism that Nkrumah warned against. "The concept of agricultural corridors," he argues, "was apparently the 'brainchild of Yara,' a major company involved in the fertilizer sector and actively involved in the foundation of the New Alliance of Food Security and Nutrition (NAFSN). The land transfers involved in such initiatives can entail massive tracts of fertile soil. Malawi alone has acquiesced to the release of 200,000 ha [hectares] under the auspices of the NAFSN."[44]

The consistent theme of African and African-descended people's land dispossession is meaningful and necessary in discourse not just about the ravages of whiteness but also about the specter of ecological destruction. Black people have suffered incredible land loss, and their potential alternative vision for the land and portions of Earth was not allowed to come to fruition. Nkrumah is particularly relevant in this regard because of his plan to create a United States of Africa. His Pan-African vision of economic and political unity among independent African countries is one that deserves reexamination in this context. Nkrumah was inspired by W. E. B. Du Bois and his leadership of Pan-African Congresses. Du Bois convinced Nkrumah that Ghana should lead a movement for Pan-Africanism, positing Pan-African socialism as the mechanism through which African nations could truly assert their independence.[45] Nkrumah's conception of "consciencism" was his expressed economic system of

---

43. Mark Langan, *Neo-colonialism and the Poverty of 'Development' in Africa* (New York: Palgrave Macmillan, 2008), 67.

44. Langan, *Neo-colonialism and the Poverty of 'Development,'* 68–69.

45. W. E. B Dubois, *The World and Africa: An Inquiry into the Part Which Africa Has Played in World History* (New York: International Publishers, 1965), 297.

choice, a slightly convoluted mixture of Western, Islamic, and traditional African values, and African socialism, rather than free-market capitalism. His vision called for African nations to control the means of production in their own states and to engage in trade, industrialize, and create viable markets among themselves to maintain a degree of independence from European and Western private and governmental actors. As a result, African nations would then be able to engage those actors from a position of economic independence and strength as opposed to dependency and patrimonialism. According to Langan,

> Nkrumah was correct to indicate that genuine, empirical sovereignty would be illusory while African countries remained "balkanized." His calls for the Union of African states—following a federal model akin to the USA—remain convincing in light of the 60 years of "development" states such as Ghana have experienced with the assistance of foreign donors and corporations. Despite the altruistic intentions which may exist among certain personnel within donor bodies (such as the European Commission), the free market prescriptions which they advance, and which their corporations enjoy, lock-in African countries into poverty and maldevelopment.[46]

Julius Nyerere, the first president of independent Tanzania, would admit years later that Nkrumah's vision of federalized African states was the most viable option for avoiding the ravages of neocolonialism, and he would express regret at his role in not fully supporting it.

---

46. Langan, *Neo-colonialism and the Poverty of 'Development'*, 271.

Kwame Nkrumah was the state crusader for African unity. He wanted the Accra Summit of 1965 to establish Union Government for the whole of independent Africa. But we failed. The one minor reason is that Kwame, like all great believers, underestimated the degree of suspicion and animosity, which his crusading passion had created among a substantial number of his fellow Heads of State. The major reason was linked to the first: already too many of us had a vested interest in keeping Africa divided.[47]

Nyerere's comments here suggest that, before Nkrumah's Pan-African vision could even get off the ground, many African leaders were already infected with the neocolonial virus, internalized whiteness, or double-consciousness (not unlike that of Rev. Daniel Payne fifty or sixty years earlier in America). The failure to enact Nkrumah's vision reveals the extent to which African elites participated in perpetuating whiteness, in furtherance of their own personal agendas and to the detriment of their own citizens and the land over which they governed.

South Africa or Azania? Disputes about Land

Nelson Mandela, the first African president of postcolonial South Africa, is viewed by those among the Black radical tradition as similarly guilty of this problem of African elites cooperating with neocolonial forces in his role in fashioning and implementing the constitution in post-apartheid South Africa. South Africa is one of the most egregious examples of white settler colonialism in Africa. Beginning in 1692, when the Dutch

---

47. Julius Nyerere, "Foreign Troops in Africa," *Africa Report* 23.4 (July–August 1978): 10–14, as quoted in Langan, *Neo-Colonialism and the Poverty of 'Development'*, 268.

arrived, the indigenous people were subject to the conquest of two invading European groups—the Dutch and the British. At odds with the English, the Boers (the Dutch) set out to expand beyond the Cape to conquer "new" lands. As Christians, they, like the Pilgrims and Puritans in the United States, appropriated the biblical narrative of the Israelites chosen by God to conquer their "promised land." Identifying with the heroes of scripture, the Dutch juxtaposed their existence as biblical Israelites against the British (as the Egyptians) and the indigenous people (as the Canaanites). Their trek across the land mass that is now South Africa and their confiscation of land and diamond mines constituted acts of forced land dispossession, reframed as a spiritual journey and God's will. The discovery of diamonds soon attracted the interest of the British who subsequently moved north, leading to the Anglo-Boer Wars.

After defeating the Boers, the British eventually established racial unity with the Dutch against the indigenous people, culminating in the system of apartheid and the creation of South Africa's version of whiteness. Whiteness always comes with land and property rights. And just as Kelly Brown Douglas describes American whiteness, whiteness in South Africa is also "the right to exclude." Apartheid resulted in even more stringent spatial containment and seizing of land from the native Africans, forcing them to become citizens of self-contained homelands and to exist in overcrowded townships. This eventually led to the rise of the Black Consciousness Movement, the development of Black theology, and international pressure to end apartheid.

Problematically, the post-apartheid constitutional democracy never sufficiently addressed the history of land dispossession nor challenged the right or assumption of white settler colonialism, and it is based on a *white historiography*. The South African Charter itself conveys its homage to whiteness when it declares,

"South Africa belongs to all who live in it, black and white." It legitimizes the white presence in South Africa without the demand for land reparations and is rooted in an ethic of racial reconciliation. While this was viewed as necessary by Mandela and other members of the African National Congress in order to quell dissension and maintain peace, the Charter itself evinces white epistemological hubris in that it never questions the presence of whites in the nation itself. Thus, in spatial terms, the post-apartheid era in South Africa is indistinguishable from that of the apartheid era.

> The majority of the people in the country, the indigenous conquered people, are still living in the same spaces, producing the same material conditions, that they did under colonialism and apartheid. It therefore follows both logically and historically that justice must be spatial and any reconciliation must be based on a spatial redivision.… With reference to the theological metaphors in the constitution, a theological agenda has already been employed to confuse the concepts of justice, liberation, and reconciliation. The theological agenda of South Africa today is one that defends and strengthens the already existing constitutional order.[48]

Azanian critical philosophy, however, challenges many of the assumptions of the post-apartheid government, the Charter, and the constitution. Azania is the proposed name of South Africa if the indigenous people were in control of their own land. It was introduced by the Pan-African Congress organized in 1959. Azanian critical philosophy emerges, therefore, as a challenge

---

48. Petrus T. Delport and Tshepo Lephakga, "Spaces of Alienation: Dispossession and Justice in South Africa," *HTS Teologiese Studies/Theological Studies* 72.1 (2016): 7.

to the assumption of white settler entitlement. The important features of this thought are the following:

1. The insistence by Azanians that the objective of the liberation struggle was the recovery of sovereign title to territory (rather than the attainment of civil and political rights).
2. The insistence that the title to territory itself belongs exclusively to the indigenous people conquered in the unjust wars of colonization.
3. The rejection of multi-racialism. This includes incredulity to the tenability of non-racialism as a means and upholding it only as an end achievable only once the title to territory has been restored to the indigenous conquered people.
4. The recognition of South Africa as a polity and idea inextricably bound to the will of the conqueror and requiring state succession by a liberated polity with a restored relationship and continuity with the rest of the African continent. This is against the political history of South Africa having constructed its identity as distinctly European and bearing no cultural resemblance and relationship with the "rest of the continent."[49]

The fourth tenet derives inspiration from Nkrumah's vision to form a federalized United States of Africa. Azanian thought raises poignant contestations about space, the territory, and who gets to control it. South Africa's attempt to construct a European identity has implications for its choice of a capitalistic economic system and its excavation of natural resources. Who is in

49. Ndumiso Dladla, "The Liberation of History and the End of South Africa: Some Notes toward an Azanian Historiography in Africa, South," *South African Journal on Human Rights* 34.3 (Dec. 31, 2018): 415–40, here 418.

control of the land and how is it being used? Azanian thought questions the historical narrative under which South Africa as a sovereign nation exists:

> South African historiography is basically white historiography since, despite its claims to "either bring black people into history" or interpret history from their vantage point, it is based on the avoidance of the right to settlement, which is in turn based on the right to conquest. As such, it is in various ways ultimately an attempt to uphold the right to conquest rather than to repudiate it.[50]

The same critique obviously could be leveled at the U.S. government and the narrative of American history in relation to the indigenous people of that land. Like Native Americans, Azanian critical philosophy makes central the problem that native Africans have been robbed of the ability to indigenize their own spaces. I maintain that Azanian thought is consistent with a broader Pan-African spatial framing and analysis across multiple countries on different continents and is critical of Black people's spatial dislocation, their rigid containment, and the conquest of their land. African-descended people have not been primary proprietors of the land and space that they should control. They have been victims of, and at times participants in, a virulent whiteness that has not only oppressed them but has eroded the land and damaged the Earth. Any theological discussions about ecological repair or recovery must address the white epistemological hubris that lies at the heart of whiteness, as manifested in these historical and current acts and practices, but that also exists within Western theology and other academic disciplines.

50. Dladla, "Liberation of History," 435.

CONVERSION BACK TO THE EARTH?

This discussion of the global history of African and African American land dispossession has been undertaken in the context of a larger discussion of the discipline of theology and its methodological limitations. These limitations manifest themselves critically in ecotheology, which calls for a radical change in the concern of theology and focus on a planetary agenda of ecological restoration. While achieving the goal of ecotheology is critically necessary and efforts to call the traditional Western theological method to account for its treatment of the Earth are admirable, much of ecotheology itself manifests white epistemological hubris in its use of traditional Western Christian logic, concepts, and discourse to solve the problem of ecocide. For example, the failure to critically interrogate the continued relevance and veracity of the idea of universal, homogeneous human sinfulness handicaps the ecotheological project and places it at odds with other theologies of liberation.

In *Ask the Beasts: Darwin and the Love of God,* Catholic feminist and ecotheologian Elizabeth A. Johnson calls for a reconceptualization of traditional Catholic theology based on the need to make impending ecological destruction the most critical concern of our time. Such a reconceptualization requires taking traditional Christian concepts and logic and reframing them to cohere with the insights of evolutionary biology, especially Darwin's theory of evolution. Conversion is one such concept that she reframes in light of the problem of ecocide. Near the end of her text, she reminds us that conversion means "literally a turning, a change of direction, switching away from one path and swiveling towards another. Accounts of religious conversion through the centuries make clear how this turning results from an awakening, slowly or abruptly, to certain spiritual realities, a new awareness that occasions changes in lifestyles, thought patterns, and moral commitments."[51] She defines conversion in this way to establish our need for a new type of conversion in light of impending ecological devastation. "We need a deep spiritual conversion to the Earth," she contends, because human beings sin "when by acts of commission, omission, or sheer indifference we disappear species, reduce biodiversity, break up integrated ecosystems, and cut off future possibilities."[52]

The Western Christian concept of "conversion" evinces the very hubris I have tried, in various ways, to explain throughout this chapter. First, who is the audience? Who is the "we" that requires a spiritual conversion to the Earth? And at what point will Christian theologians account for silenced and repressed voices and paradigms, deemed primitive and uncivilized by Western Christian missionaries, clerics, scholars, and colonial agents, which are consistent with the perspective Johnson, among others, now endorses? Because she is bound by the language and logic of traditional Christian discourse, Johnson both falsely universalizes the situation of sin characterized by ecocide and fails to acknowledge how the language of conversion historically has been used as a tool of oppression against African-descended peoples.

I have chronicled at length in my earlier work how traditional Protestant Christian discourse about the need for conversion was used in an oppressive way to convince African-descended people of their innate inferiority.[53] Christian conversion narratives of enslaved Africans in America followed a consistent pattern of first "a feeling of sinfulness, then a vision of damna-

51. Elizabeth A. Johnson, *Ask the Beasts: Darwin and the God of Love* (London: Bloomsbury, 2014), 257.

52. Johnson, *Ask the Beasts*, 258.

53. Jawanza Eric Clark, *Indigenous Black Theology: Toward an African-Centered Theology of the African American Religious Experience* (New York: Palgrave Macmillan, 2012).

tion, and finally an experience of unconditional election."[54] I argued that their "feeling of sinfulness" was based on a feeling of racial sinfulness derived from having been brought from Africa in chains and convinced of their prior primitive (read sinful) African existence. George Kelsey rightly noted that B\lack people were victims of a "double fall," both the universal fall of all humanity and an added racial fall as African-descended people.[55] Their distance from Africa and literal movement west correlates to their perceived proximity to and from the truth, enlightenment, and proper religious awareness. The history of this deracinated cultural distortion and internalized whiteness among Black people is not addressed at all in Johnson's invocation of the term, which makes her claims of the need to convert to the Earth all the more ironic.

Historically, white missionaries and colonizers encouraged, and in some instances forced, African and African-descended people's conversion to traditional Western Christianity. This conversion was a simultaneous conversion away from the Earth, away from their traditional African worldview, and away from their traditional religious perspective viewed then as heathen and ungodly. Their worldview valued the Earth and viewed the land as an extension of human life itself, the home of ancestors and other powerful spiritual agents. It called them to seek harmony and to be reconciled with nature, and to maintain balance between themselves, other living creatures, and the rest of the natural world. It is a worldview rooted in interrelationship. "I am because we are, and because we are therefore I am." This is "the path they switched from" in order to come under "a

54. Clark, *Indigenous Black Theology*, 26.
55. George D. Kelsey, *Racism and the Christian Understanding of Man: An Analysis and Criticism of Racism as an Idolatrous Religion* (New York: Scribner, 1965), 26.

new [Christian] awareness." This "path," or worldview, was also the hallmark and prevailing influence over Nkrumah's effort to create a Pan-African federation of states in postcolonial Africa. To be asked now to convert back to the Earth is presumptuous and arrogant.

Johnson manifests aspects of white hubris because her challenge fails to account for the way traditional white Christian logic and rhetoric are, themselves, implicated in the worldview of those promoting racial oppression and effecting impending ecological destruction. The very language she employs is part of the problem. Her use of the all-encompassing "we"—as in "we need a deep spiritual conversion to the Earth"—manifests the hubris that indicates knowledge is objectively true only when white Christians confirm it as such. Her description of how this conversion reveals itself intellectually, emotionally, and ethically involves epistemological and philosophical features of the very African and Native American worldviews that previous white Catholic and Protestant perspectives deemed primitive and uncivilized.

Johnson presents a theocentric, as opposed to an anthropocentric, view of the world and the notion of the self as not isolated but interconnected to other living creatures and the rest of nature as radical theological ideas, without the least bit of irony. These perspectives were subjugated in the name of a white, capitalistic patriarchy, which was globalized, and now the very ideas derived from that perspective are touted as the solution to the restoration of the Earth. No conversion to the Earth can occur without, first, a conversion away from whiteness and the hubris implicit in its prevailing assumptions. No conversion to the Earth can take place without taking account of the dead bodies and blood-soaked spaces of Earth that call out for a memorial. We do not need a conversion to the Earth. We need to reclaim stolen Earth. We need spatial healing and recovery. This begins with a reconsideration of the way we think about and access God and God's power. How might we construct a Pan-African doctrine of God that prioritizes the space and land? It is to this question that I now turn.

3

A Pan-African Conception of God

The methodological shift to a spatially oriented theology calls for a radical reassessment of the Black Protestant Christian conception of God. Chapter 2 described the difference between the indigenous African conception of land and the white Western perspective. The history of Black land dispossession in America is a story about Black people's often unsuccessful attempts to Africanize/indigenize the spaces they inhabit. Relegation to spatial constriction and confinement is a consequence and element of racial oppression and also has implications for the impending threat of ecological destruction. Critical to recovery and restoration is reexamining the way we conceptualize God. I contend that the God-symbol that most promotes spatial recovery and ecological healing is one derived from African mysticism that is a symbol simultaneously useful in healing the spiritual and spatial divide between African Americans and continental Africans.

The God of classical theism, the dominant God-symbol of the Western Christian tradition, is a conception of divinity rooted in a temporal orientation that, while resilient, has consistently helped propagate oppressive realities. This God is defined as the God of the alpha and the omega, a God of perfect goodness, and its prominent metaphor is that of king and/or father. Traditional notions of providence and eschatology derive from this temporal fixation. God knows the beginning but also the end-times, and as "He" is also perfect goodness, this God manifests outcomes within that presumed perfect goodness. Black, feminist, and Womanist theologians and ecotheologians have long criticized this conception/symbol and its role in the perpetuation of racial and gender oppression and in justification of destruction of the Earth.

Yet most of these same theologians have failed to consider how a God construct framed within a temporal orientation also continues the perpetuation of theological ideas that result in a continued alienation from the natural world, while rendering invisible the trauma incurred by Black people's spatial dislocation and geographical rupture and confinement. An anthropomorphic and anthropocentric conception of God (God in the form of a human being whose primary concerns are those of human beings) has been deleterious to oppressed humanity and the rest of the Earth. It is not just detrimental because this conception is sexist and misogynist—or because ecotheologians critique it as the God-symbol most instrumental in perpetuating a dominion paradigm that reduces the Earth to an object of human manipulation—but because acceptance of this type of God-symbol also reveals the ways in which various forms of liberation theology continue to be trapped within a Western temporal paradigm centered on notions of human progress, ultimately limiting their theological potential and conceptual possibilities.

Which God-symbol, or conception of God, is most useful in Africanizing current spaces in order to heal the Earth? I am particularly focused on the theological limitations evinced by Black theology, given its reluctance to embrace conceptual contributions derived from traditional African spirituality. Were Black theologians to reject their own double-consciousness and embrace aspects of the African mystical tradition within their construction of the doctrine of God, it would both affirm the critiques of classical theism put forth by Black, feminist, and Womanist scholars and provide a conception of the divine capable of addressing the trauma incurred by African-descended people's spatial dislocation and legacy of rigid geographical containment and alienation from the Earth. Part of this work involves embracing a notion of God that can heal the divide and collapse the spatial distance that exists between continental Africans and African Americans, among other diasporic Africans. We can begin to heal the divide by overcoming the alienation generated by double-consciousness, a problem shared across the spatial terrain of the Atlantic.

Double-Consciousness:
A Transatlantic Phenomenon

In 1901, the famed sociologist and theorist W. E. B. Du Bois defined *double-consciousness* as "this sense of always looking at oneself through the eyes of another … a two-ness, an American, a Negro, two warring ideals in one dark body whose dogged strength alone keeps it from being torn asunder."[1] For Du Bois, double-consciousness is the consequence of racialization. It is the projection of inferiority on the Black body, the perception of blackness, and black Africanness, as primitive and in need of cultivation. This second-sight is the perception of the self through a veil, the creation of "the Negro." Africana scholars refer to this perception problem as "negrification." Albert Cleage Jr. described the process as "niggerization." Frantz Fanon, writing in the Afro-Caribbean and African context, agreed with

---

1. W. E. B Du Bois, *The Souls of Black Folk* (Chicago: A. C. McClurg, 1903).

Du Bois, arguing that Black/African people continue to view themselves as a problem and in so doing continue to manifest double-consciousness. Fanon explains that this consciousness results from the pressure to satisfy a white, or European, norm as the measure of what constitutes human.

> In other words, I began to suffer from not being a white man to the degree that the white man imposes discrimination on me, makes me a colonized native, robs me of all worth, all individuality, tells me that I am a parasite on the world, that I must bring myself as quickly as possible into step with the white world.… Then I will quite simply try to make myself white: that is, I will compel the white man to acknowledge that I am human.[2]

Second-sight, or double-consciousness, within the Black person, then, is the white gaze upon the Black self. It is Black antiblackness and Black anti-Africanness, black skin, and white masks. Double-consciousness prevents an authentic self-consciousness.

Du Bois and Fanon describe a problem that was, in the twentieth century, and continues to be in the twenty-first, a *transcontextual* concern. It is transcontinental, a diasporic phenomenon. By this I mean that continental Africans and diasporic Africans, specifically African Americans, share the experience of double-consciousness, which at its core is the problem of African-descended people's acceptance of their own cultural and religious inferiority relative to the West, Western culture, and Western productions of knowledge. This feeling of inferiority evinces an internal conflict, two warring ideals. These ideals are conflictive thought forms, or paradigms, and combative world-

---

2. Frantz Fanon, *Black Skin, White Masks* (Paris: Editions du Seuil, 1952), 98.

views. Western Christianity and specific Western theological claims and methodological approaches are central to this problem because religion often has been the primary vehicle, transporter, and disseminator of the Western worldview accepted by African peoples, particularly in the United States and in West Africa.

Black theology posits itself as a theology of resistance to white theology and has for over fifty years called out the racism of white American theology. In so doing, it has been highly influential in paving the way for new theologies to emerge, such as Womanist theology in North America, Black theology in South Africa and Great Britain, Minjung theology in Korea, and Dalit theology in India. James Cone is arguably the most influential and productive American theologian of the twentieth and early twenty-first centuries. His development of Black theology and voluminous publication record have been essential in providing Black theology with academic legitimacy, greatly influencing the cultivation of seminary-trained pastors. I argue, however, that Black theology's inability to establish itself as truly independent of whiteness and the white academic norms it condemns is a clear limitation of the project or subfield. The reification of blackness within the project itself, in the form of *ontological blackness*, has made it less appealing to continental Africans, for example, and has made collaboration between U.S. Black theologians and African theologians tense and difficult over the years. I contend that ontological blackness not only fails to resolve double-consciousness but is itself a manifestation of double-consciousness or second-sight. Similarly, African theology, with a few noteworthy exceptions, has been inhibited by its acceptance of a Eurocentric definition of revelation and has tended to force traditional African religious symbols and idioms to conform to a Eurocentric Christian norm.

However, two postcolonial African-centered theologians, one in the United States and one in Ghana, have constructed creative Black theologies, uninhibited by a Eurocentric methodology and traditional Western Christian commitments, that attempt to resolve double-consciousness and provide a program for Black liberation/social transformation by incorporating what I call an *Africana theological methodology* rooted in a pantheistic notion of the oneness of God, or God as a unifying power, energy, spirit, and intelligence. Albert Cleage Jr. and Ishmael Tetteh each construct a type of African-centered, spatial theology that resists reification of race, exclusivist truth claims, or an anthropomorphic conception of God. Their identical doctrine of God provides the link, or bridge, that manifests a transcontextual or Pan-African consciousness and posits a God construct that offers a path toward spatial reconciliation and recovery and also shares much with ecotheological models of God. Their theologies provide a way forward for Black theology, one that is rhetorically a theology of liberation, unencumbered by double-consciousness and, specifically, the need to conform to white academic norms or to be subject to white (or Black) theological policing. Each pastor theologian intends the practitioner to cultivate a God consciousness that incorporates principles of African mysticism within the doing of what could be a Pan-African, Eco-Black, or Africana spatial theology. This process involves encouraging the seeker to activate their God power, or inner divinity, becoming one's true self by *plugging in* or increasing one's connection to the divine power source.

What emerges is neither traditional Black theology, African theology, nor an uncritical hermeneutic of return to traditional African religions, in large part because they shun exclusivism and embrace idioms, religious practices, and technologies that derive from various religious traditions. The result is

a creolized, hybrid theology that resists classical categorization
or traditional systematization but evinces the traditional African methodological approach often characterized by Western
scholars as "endless elasticity."[3] It is an African-inspired spatial
theology rooted in a conception of God as the one that fills
and energizes all the places in which we gather. The theology's
openness to modalities of other religions stems from a symbol
of God as energy, power, and creative intelligence, a conception
that subverts and avoids the problem Tillich identifies as idolatry: when the religious becomes demonic, or more specifically
what Eboussi Boulaga refers to as the "fetishism of revelation."[4]
These theologians invite Black theology to become more African-centered and, given their respective contexts, constitute a
type of Pan-African, or Africana, theology.

Black Theology and Second-Sight

Josiah Young has written extensively on existential realities
that North American Blacks and Black Africans share in his
construction of a Pan-African theology. He proposes that these
groups engage in a transcontextual dialogue to construct a theology that "seeks to valorize what blacks have in common: African descent, cultural modalities, and especially among the poor,
radical similarity in socioeconomic suffering."[5] For Young,
transcontextual consciousness eventually inspires development
of one of possibly many Pan-African theologies and is primar-

---

3. Stephen R. Prothero, *God Is Not One: The Eight Rival Religions That
Run the World—and Why Their Differences Matter* (New York: HarperOne,
2010), 231.

4. F. Eboussi Boulaga, *Christianity without Fetishes: An African Critique
and Recapture of Christianity* (Maryknoll, NY: Orbis Books, 1981), 11.

5. Josiah Ulysses Young III, *A Pan-African Theology: Providence and the
Legacies of the Ancestors* (Trenton, NJ: Africa World Press, 1992), 11.

ily informed by the experience shared by blacks, especially the poor, of oppression and the struggle for liberation from oppression imposed by a white, capitalistic, Christian hegemony. Pan-African theology is formed by the dictates of Black religion, and, while it may be significantly Christian, it need not be defined exclusively by Christian symbols. Young's focus on socioeconomic suffering or poverty is critical, and I applaud his insistence on prioritizing the most marginalized and vulnerable populations as he develops a theology whose first commitment is to praxis. I argue, however, that double-consciousness should be added to the list of elements that Blacks in the Americas and continental Africans, particularly sub-Saharan, have in common. Double-consciousness (or second-sight) warrants critical religio-cultural analysis as an element of transcontextual consciousness. In fact, this problem of second-sight afflicts the Black/African middle and upper classes as much as the poor and is a category that must be engaged within the development of any Pan-African theology. Critical engagement with theology is crucial and necessary here since the Christianization process has been integral to the cultivation of double-consciousness both in the Americas and in Africa.

African American and Black African conversion to and embrace of Western Christianity inculcates double-consciousness. It does this by way of Western Christianity's absolute truth claims and forced rupture with the religious orientation or worldview that preceded it—the indigenous African worldview with its particular theological prerogatives. Conversion is understood as a turning away from the African religious past, even a wholesale rejection of it. Absolute Christian truth claims cultivate alienation from that ancestral past and pose as the superior orientation and ultimate way of being or form of truth. Acceptance of this exclusivist posture inevitably leads to

a self-alienation, which facilitates double-consciousness or second-sight. In an earlier work, I describe this process as manifesting anti-African sentiment in Black Christians, specifically in
America but also in West Africa.[6] Eboussi Boulaga argues,

> All the Christianities have the *form of certitude.* Each
> is sure of its facts and cannot admit that it may have
> been wrong. For each, the multiplicity of content, or of
> Christianities, is nonsense, because only one is true and
> the others are false. Each is absolute, convinced that its
> categories are true and its ways of acting best suited for
> all humanity.[7]

Boulaga points out what is empirically obvious, that there
are varieties, or versions, of Christianity with hundreds of Protestant denominations in Africa and America alone. Each Christianity, however, presents itself as theologically absolute despite
its sociological or practical relativity. Such theological absolutism, primarily achieved through the theological idea of revelation, rejects all other ways of knowing and being and helps bring
about second-sight in the colonized, whose first-sight consists of
ways of knowing and being that contradict this presumption.

Boulaga goes on to describe the Western/European missionary Christian view of revelation as fetish religion. In so doing,
he applies the category "fetish," invented by Europeans to dis-
parage African people, to Western Christianity and invites us to
interrogate the limitations of both the doctrine of revelation and
the traditional Western conception of God. Historically, Europeans have used the category "fetish" in a derogatory manner

---

6. Jawanza Eric Clark, *Indigenous Black Theology: Toward an African-
Centered Theology of the African-American Religious Experience* (New York:
Palgrave Macmillan, 2012).

7. Boulaga, *Christianity without Fetishes,* 6 (italics in original).

to dismiss traditional African religious practices as magic and superstition. According to William Pietz, this concept originated in the sixteenth and seventeenth centuries on the West African coast, where Europeans condemned Africans' manner of attributing value, agency, and power to material things. The fetish is irreducibly material.[8] The Western theological paradigm necessitated the invention of the fetish and the categorization of indigenous African religions as fetish religion. The fetish as pejorative represents a marker of inferiority; it names the primitive, the magical, and the irrational. Fetish religion marks the practitioners of indigenous African religions as inferior, as believers in superstition. It is a category invented to validate the European colonial project and to justify European/Western Christian imperialism. As such the category fetish continues to portray indigenous Africa and traditional African religions as a negative symbol in the consciousness of Black Christians. Sylvester Johnson states, "The fetish became not only the established synecdoche for African indigenous religions but also the most potent intellectual category for the colonial enterprise of interpreting and studying religion comparatively."[9] It was the concept that Europeans/Westerners used to judge and delineate legitimate religious expressions and modalities from illegitimate ones, truth from falsehood. In *The Fetish Revisited*, J. Lorand Matory claims,

> What makes a fetish a fetish is not its falsity but the context of intercultural, interclass, intergender, and inter-

---

8. William Pietz, "The Problem of the Fetish, I," in *Anthropology and Aesthetics*, ed. Francesco Pellizzi (Chicago: University of Chicago Press, 1985), 7.

9. Sylvester A. Johnson, *African American Religions, 1500–2000: Colonialism, Democracy, and Freedom* (Cambridge: Cambridge University Press, 2015), 58.

personal controversy and contestation that leads some
people to call the thing a fetish (in Hegel's, Marx's, or
Freud's sense), while other people call it a true god, a
true spirit, a true repository of value or agency, or an
authentic metonym of some real force that matters.[10]

He goes on to state that, for Europeans, fetishes "are objects
onto which people have falsely projected value, agency, or
authenticity that truly belong elsewhere."[11] In using the term to
describe traditional Western Christian theological approaches,
Boulaga effectively exposes the ways in which Western Christianity evinces white epistemological hubris.

The positivism of the Christian revelation, whether regarding
the Bible itself or Jesus's life and his death on the cross, functions as what Boulaga calls a "fetishism of revelation," creating an idol, an absolutized symbol, that is used as a weapon of
imperialism through missionary activity when imposed on the
unconverted. The image of Christ, the cross, and the Bible are
now God objectified, or God in material form, capable of defin-
ing winners and losers, those chosen for salvation and those condemned to eternal hellfire. This fetishizing impulse, however,
actually stems from the way we conceptualize God as a simultaneously transcendent and immanent being with agency. So,
certain Christian symbols become fetishes because an agential
God is believed to be subsumed within these objects, which are
then used to theologically terrorize and manipulate the colonized all over the world. Boulaga asks, "Why, indeed, has it
been thought that a positivism, or fetishism, of revelation can
be avoided in fixing God's manifestation not in a piece of wood

---

10. J. Lorand Matory, *The Fetish Revisited: Marx, Freud, and the Gods
Black People Make* (Durham, NC: Duke University Press, 2018), 31.
    11. Matory, *Fetish Revisited*, 31.

but in a slice of time—two thousand years, or thirty years?"[12] All salvific truth and significant divine activity are apparently subsumed in this one event. Boulaga continues,

> They will tell us with all assurance that God has acted with such-and-such an intention, or at such-and-such a moment in history, even in their own lives. What persuades them that they have abandoned metaphorical language when they pretend to be privy to the express will, the "customary ways," of God? Do they mean they might possess the knowledge he has of himself, the world, and the human being?[13]

Both the West African and the African American Christian, having no prior exposure to Christianity before conversion by white missionaries, fell prey to this process. Thus, they fell victim to the tendency of Christianity to function and perpetuate "imperialism as a discursive field of knowledge."[14]

Black Theology's Fetishism of Biblical Revelation

Black theology, despite James Cone's insistence that it must conform to the dictates of its African heritage and not European enslavement, continues to fetishize the revelation of Christ and, by extension, God; and, in so doing, fails to resolve the problem of second-sight, instead exhibiting the residual effects of it. Black theology correctly identifies whiteness, or the ideology of white supremacy, as the problem with American Christianity or white theology. Cone calls whiteness the Antichrist. Yet he clings to a

---

12. Boulaga, *Christianity without Fetishes,* 12.
13. Boulaga, *Christianity without Fetishes*, 12.
14. Boulaga, *Christianity without Fetishes*, 21.

reified notion of blackness even when blackness is created from whiteness because of the theological centrality of the revelation of Jesus Christ. It is the problem of ontological blackness. Other Black theologians and scholars of religions have made this critique of Black theology. My point here is to demonstrate how specific claims about God, specifically that God is on the side of the oppressed, both reflect double-consciousness and represent a fetishism of revelation and specific biblical narratives.

Black theology, specifically ontological blackness, manifests double-consciousness in failing to transcend racialization since "both black suffering and rebellion are ontologically created and provoked by whiteness as a necessary condition of blackness."[15] This is why Victor Anderson describes Black theology as a "crisis theology" or a theology in "a crisis of legitimation."[16] Black theology fetishizes revelation by presenting itself as a theology of liberation yet appearing to be most vehemently concerned with maintaining its Christian bona fides. This is clearly seen in the debate between James Cone and William Jones regarding the question of God's role in Black suffering, or theodicy in Black theology.

In 1973, William Jones provided perhaps the most trenchant and insightful critique of Black theology when he raised the issue of theodicy in Black suffering. In his provocatively named *Is God a White Racist?*, Jones proposed a challenge to the fundamental claim of Black theology, the claim that God is good and on the side of the oppressed.[17] Jones reasoned that such a claim had to be demonstrated or proven and not simply presupposed

15. Victor Anderson, "Ontological Blackness in Theology," in *African-American Religious Thought: An Anthology*, ed. Cornel West and Eddie S. Glaude Jr. (Louisville: Westminster John Knox Press, 2003), 897.

16. Anderson, "Ontological Blackness in Theology," 906.

17. William R. Jones, *Is God a White Racist? A Preamble to Black Theology* (Boston: Beacon Press, 1973).

or stated as a given, especially considering the history of the multigenerational and international reality of Black subjugation and oppression. Historical, even empirical, evidence suggests that, because Black oppression continues, theologians might have to conclude God is a white racist given the global existential condition of African-descended peoples. Another way of framing Jones's concern is to say he is worried that Cone might be fetishizing a certain biblical conception of God. Is the claim that God is on the side of the oppressed, despite the lack of historical evidence, not assigning value and agency to a material thing: the Bible? Does it not subsume God within interpretations of primarily two biblical narratives: the exodus and Jesus events? Jones, of course, does not conclude that God is in fact a white racist, but he merely raises the question so that Black theologians may develop theologies that can properly refute such a claim.

Almost fifty years later, however, the question remains whether Black theology ever provided an adequate response to Jones. Anthony Pinn would answer no. Even now, Black and Womanist theologies remain silent or fail to appreciate the way their doctrine of God is really what Pinn would call "a weak humanism."[18] At the heart of William Jones's concern is whether Black theology, even after rejecting white theology, still retained a residue of the oppressor's worldview in its theology, specifically as evident in its doctrine of God. Jones appeared to be worried about double-consciousness and the question of whether the development of Black theology was in fact being informed by second-sight. Put another way, he was concerned that Black theology, while ostensibly rejecting racism and whiteness, still relied on categories and theological representations that derived

---

18. Anthony B. Pinn, *The End of God-Talk: An African American Humanist Theology* (Oxford: Oxford University Press, 2012), 148.

from a Eurocentric paradigm, most clearly in its acceptance of a Eurocentric construction of God (combining both Hebrew and Greek constructs), and thus was responsive to and continually developing itself as reactionary to the foil of whiteness.

Linda Tuhiwai Smith warns of this in her discussion of the negative impact of Western research methodologies on indigenous peoples of the world. She describes double-consciousness by another name while retaining the emphasis on and metaphor of sight. This approach asks the question, Why are indigenous peoples around the world judging themselves through the gaze or lens of the colonizer? Concerned that such a preoccupation places limitations on these peoples' ability to reach self-actualization, Smith notes:

> This sense of what the idea of the West represents is important here because to a large extent theories about research are underpinned by a cultural system of classification and representation, by views about human nature, human morality and virtue, by conceptions of space and time, by conceptions of gender and race. Ideas about these things help determine what counts as real. Systems of classifications and representation enable different traditions or fragments of traditions to be retrieved and reformulated in different contexts as discourses, and then to be played out in systems of power and domination, with real material consequences for colonized peoples.[19]

The question within the discipline of theology is, What is allowed to "count as real," or, in the case of Black theology,

---

19. Linda Tuhiwai Smith, *Decolonizing Methodologies: Research and Indigenous Peoples* (London: Zed Books, 1999), 44.

as legitimately Christian? And might not the "systems of clas-sifications and representation" place shackles on the possibil-ity of actualizing liberation through Black theology? In other words, is Christian systemization more important than actual Black liberation? William Jones's critique is, at heart, a critique of theological method. He thought the Christian conception of God itself inhibited the possibility of a truly Black theology of liberation. Jones contends that "the initial task of the black theo-logian is to liberate the black mind from the destructive ideas and submissive attitudes that checkmate any movement toward authentic emancipation. It is to effect what I term the gnosio-logical conversion of the black psyche.… Gnosiological conver-sion, in the black context, reduces to the 'deniggerification' of blacks."[20] While Jones takes various Black theologians to task, including Albert Cleage Jr., Major Jones, and J. Deotis Rob-erts, James Cone, to his credit, provided a published response to Jones's critique of him. Cone's response, however, warrants reflection, and I argue that it conveys evidence of second-sight or double-consciousness.

Jones's critique of Cone stems from Cone's reliance on the redemptive suffering theodicy, based on Christ's suffering on the cross, his death, and resurrection. Jesus's triumph over death is an indication that Blacks will be liberated from oppression as they suffer in the struggle for that liberation. Jones, however, is critical of the concept of redemptive suffering, because the claim cannot be asserted while the suffering is happening but only ret-rospectively after some event of liberation (i.e., the resurrection). This is why theologians often refer to Jesus Christ's suffering on the cross as an example of prima facie evil and not genuine evil. What appeared to be evil at first glance was proven to be neces-sary, according to traditional Christian theology, to bring about

---

20. Jones, *Is God a White Racist?*, 67.

a greater good (the resurrection and redemption of humanity) in hindsight. The problem with applying this logic to the situation of Black oppression in America is that Black oppression continues. Therefore, unless Cone can definitively point to an actual event of liberation, or exaltation/resurrection, that can be used to retrospectively vindicate the multigenerational oppression and suffering of Black people, his theology has not eliminated the prospect of divine racism. The debate is also clearly entrenched in a temporal orientation requiring some future liberatory event to prove past events of racial suffering necessary or meaningful. Such an orientation fails to adequately evaluate or assess the current moment in the hope that some future event will redeem past suffering.

Cone's response to Jones's critique refers back to the resurrection of Jesus Christ as the definitive event of Black liberation. In so doing, Cone demonstrates how his theology succumbs to Boulaga's "fetishism of revelation" critique by confining God's agency and activity to a specific "slice of time." We must also ask if, in his exclusive focus on the cross, he is not assigning *value, agency, and authenticity* that more properly should be assigned elsewhere. What is curious about his response is that the resurrection of Jesus Christ, historically speaking, obviously precedes the modern era and specifically the beginning of the transatlantic slave trade, the start of the Maafa. Further, unlike Cleage, Cone does not view Jesus or the biblical Israelites as necessarily racially Black. As a result, it is hard to see how this is a proper example or sufficient evidence of Black liberation or an adequate response to the questions raised by Jones. It is an answer that Cone knows, and even states explicitly, is unacceptable to Jones. But "in responding to Jones, Christian theologians have to admit that their logic is not the same as other forms of rational discourse. The coming of God in Jesus breaks open history and thereby creates an experience of truth-encounter that makes us talk in ways not often understandable to those who have not had the experience."[21] Cone turns revelation into a fetish and then uses it as a trump card, a cudgel, to explain why his theology is exempt from the criticism Jones makes and, furthermore, why Jones will not understand it. Even more confounding, he states that most Black people are Christian and not secular humanists and that, thus, his argument is likely to be more persuasive, and apparently more popular, than Jones's (which are humanist), as humanism cannot offer the hope that Christian acceptance of God's mystery can.

Cone's response here is a problematic framing of Christian logic as oppositional to secular humanist logic. Such framing implies that a religionist, in this case a Christian, and a secular humanist cannot engage in meaningful dialogue on the question of Black suffering and God's role in it, because humanists do not believe in God. Cone fails to acknowledge, however, that Jones offered his critique from within the discursive frame of God-talk, or at least the presumption of theism, and actually proposed *humanocentric theism* as an alternative doctrine of God and possible solution to his concern about divine racism. Cone's failure to address Jones's proposed doctrine of God speaks to the extent to which Black theology is mostly concerned with being a work of Christian apologetics rather than an actual theology of liberation. Cone changes the subject to a debate between theism and atheism, knowing that most Blacks, even those who are not traditional Protestant Christians, still tend to be theists. This subtle avoidance of Jones's actual argument reveals that Cone is intent on defending the absolutism of Christ even when alternative theological possibilities are presented to him. Would most

---

21. James H. Cone, *God of the Oppressed* (New York: Seabury Press, 1975), 176.

Blacks agree that "this faith in Jesus' victory over suffering is a once-and-for-all event of liberation" when Black oppression continues despite acceptance of Christianity by the majority of continental and diasporic Africans?[22] Whence the phrase *once-and-for-all*? Cone appears to prove Jones's thesis that the oppressor's residue resides within Black theology, and to confirm Boulaga's concern about Western Christianity's tendency to fetishize a particular biblical conception of God through revelation.

Anthony Pinn has championed Jones's criticism perhaps more than any other Black theologian. He goes further than Jones, not only accusing Black and Womanist theologies, but even Jones's own proposal of "humanocentric theism," as versions of weak humanism. Pinn argues that "black and womanist theologies argue for weak humanism in that they give so much weight to the doctrine of God understood through the humanization of God in the Christ Event, with a sense of real optimism premised on the presence of God in the struggle for liberation."[23] Pinn's argument, like that of other Western secular humanists who argue against the existence of God, seems trapped in Western religious categories and grammar. He, like Cone, reduces this discussion to a juxtaposition between Christian theism and secular humanism, as if those are the only two options. Either God is objectified in a human being, Jesus Christ, which invariably leads to the claim that theology is anthropology, or weak humanism, or God does not exist and human beings are functionally responsible for the human condition and all human outcomes. What is missing are the myriad of alternative conceptions of God, specifically those of African mysticism, that do not reify God in a human being. Cone, Jones, and Pinn write

22. Cone, *God of the Oppressed*, 177.
23. Pinn, *End of God-Talk,* 148.

extensively about African Americans and their struggle to over-come racial oppression, yet all three are reluctant to turn toward African thought systems in order to recover alternative symbols, idioms, or technologies potentially useful in shaping a theology of Black liberation.

In this sense, their words convey V. Nandy's contention that "colonization functions as a 'shared culture' for those who have been colonized and for those who have colonized. This means, for example, that colonized peoples share a language of coloni-zation, share knowledge about their colonizers, and, in terms of a political project, share the same struggle for decolonization."[24] Here I am describing Christian systematic theology and theo-dicy discourse as a language of colonization for Black people, especially those academically and denominationally trained, centered on Christology. Black systematic theologians represent Gramscian "traditional intellectuals," who are tied to the institu-tions and apparatus of the state, or status quo.[25] Consequently, they manifest second-sight and are precluded from prioritizing or centering new and/or culturally diverse formations, ideas, or modalities that would foreground the goal of Black liberation over Christian apologetics. For the person of African descent, this theological language of colonization specifically forecloses the possibility of indigenous African or African-influenced religious formations or conceptions that antedate conversion to Christianity from being incorporated within a Black, or an Africana, theology. This places Black theology in a conceptual box from which it has yet to break free.

24. Smith, *Decolonizing Methodologies*, 45.

25. Antonio Gramsci, *Selections from the Prison Notebooks of Antonio Gramsci*, ed. and trans. Quintin Hoare and Geoffrey Nowell Smith (New York: International Publishers, 1971), 14.

Ecotheology and God

Ecotheologians have been less dependent on classical conceptions of God because of the urgency to deconstruct harmful theological ideas that may contribute to ecological destruction. Some ecotheologians, for example, argue for a pantheist or panentheistic conception of God as they challenge the traditional view of God as an agential Supreme Being. Some of these alternative models are a step in the right direction, even if not entirely satisfactory. Sallie McFague's ecological theology maintains that the model of God as king must be rejected in favor of an organic model akin to viewing the Earth/universe as the body of God. She claims that these models are at odds precisely because of how people conceptualize an agential God. In prioritizing God's independent agency, the classical Western tradition heavily emphasized God's transcendence and utter freedom over God's immanence. The model of the universe as God's body, she thinks, may overemphasize God's immanence and, as in pantheism, completely rejects God's transcendence. In pantheism, the universe is God. This means that human beings and all the creatures and living realities that reside therein are a part of God. Of course, the classical Western tradition has a long history of casting disdain on the idea of pantheism, usually because it sees pantheism as not acknowledging sufficiently the depth and power of sin and evil nor sufficiently distinguishing a good God from evil, sinful matter. McFague acknowledges the limitations of pantheism and is in search of an even better metaphor that combines organic and agential models in a way that enables us to see our interconnection and interdependency with the rest of the natural world and to accept our place within the ecosystem.

McFague settles on the conception of God as the spirit, or the breath, that animates the body and gives it life. "If the model were that God is related to the world as spirit is related to body, perhaps the values of both the agential and organic models could be preserved."[26] She calls this new model a *spirit theology*, which she thinks dislodges *anthropocentrism* in favor of *cosmocentrism*. As McFague explains,

> A spirit theology suggests another possibility: that God is not primarily the orderer and controller of the universe but its source and empowerment, the breath that enlivens and energizes it. The spirit perspective takes seriously the fecundity, diversity, range, and complexity of life and of life supporting systems. It does not claim that the divine mind is the cause of what evolutionary theory tells us can have only local causes; rather, it suggests that we think of these local causes as enlivened and empowered by the breath of God.[27]

What I find intriguing about McFague's formulation is the extent of its similarities to an African mystical conception of divine power. She goes on to assert that her conception is consistent with, and not oppositional to, contemporary science and is the most pragmatic model for addressing the problem of impending ecological destruction. The breath or spirit is akin to a power source that not only connects all living things but also powers up and gives life to all living things. Here again, ecotheologians provide a solution to a problem that white epistemological hubris prevents them from seeing, a solution that has always existed as an active cultural modality but has been suppressed by the subjugation of oppressed people's perspectives and theological contributions. What McFague is describing is the very "conjurational spirituality" described in chapter 1 that

26. Sallie McFague, *Models of God: Theology for an Ecological, Nuclear Age* (Philadelphia: Fortress Press, 1987), 141.

27. McFague, *Models of God*, 145.

derives from indigenous African spirituality. Images of God as the power source and creative energy and intelligence that gives us life are God-symbols that are both ecologically necessary and essential in addressing the problem of African-descended people's second-sight. It is a step in the right direction.

However, McFague is not committed to the metaphor of spirit or breath. She, like other ecotheologians, is insistent on drawing a clear distinction between pantheism and panentheism and making clear that panentheism is the preferred option. For the former, the universe is God; but, for the latter, the universe is inside of God but not the totality of God. McFague explains panentheism this way: "God as the spirit is the source, the life, the breath of all reality. Everything that is is *in* God and God is *in* all things and yet God is not identical with the universe, for the universe is dependent on God in a way that God is not dependent on the universe."[28] McFague is clearly committed to establishing God's independence of the all/world/universe. But why is it necessary to assert God's independence of the universe when the universe is not a finite reality but an infinite one? The difference between pantheism and panentheism is an abstract, conceptual distinction that makes no practical or tangible difference. Yet panentheism provides a way for various ecotheologians to hold on to an attenuated notion of transcendence and agency that aligns closer with Hebrew and Christian biblical God-symbols. In this way, some ecotheologians compromise and end up promoting ideas that do not fit precisely with their stated objectives and agenda. The promotion of panentheism over pantheism is not for the purposes of prioritizing a radical planetary agenda but is merely a homage to Christian apologetics. Inspired by the theologies of two Pan-African organic intellectuals, I argue for an African mystical conception of God that is both pantheistic and amoral.

28. McFague, *Models of God*, 149.

This God is a neutral power that provides the energy to make things happen. As the Akan of Ghana say, "If you want to talk to God, speak to the winds."

Pan-African Organic Intellectuals

Transgressing the boundaries of Christian theological systematization, specifically as it concerns the doctrine of God, opens possibilities for transcending double-consciousness, prioritizing the goals of liberation and ecological healing, and bridging the spatial chasm that exists between Africans and African Americans. Two theologians, Albert Cleage Jr. in North America and Ishmael Tetteh in Ghana, West Africa, take William Jones's concern seriously and go further than ecotheologians by incorporating African mysticism within their doctrine of God and their respective Africana theologies. These pastor theologians, whom I refer to as Gramscian *organic intellectuals*, construct novel African-centered spatial theologies that are pragmatic in their goal of spiritual, social, and political transformation.

Cornel West was the first to make the case that Antonio Gramsci's Marxist philosophy has usefulness to Black theologians who claim *liberation* as the telos of their theologies. West has long lamented that Black theology seems unwilling to engage in serious class analysis or to offer stringent critiques of capitalism and its global effects on oppressed Black people in America, in Africa, and throughout the African diaspora (I will address this in more detail in chapter 5). West recommends analysis of Gramsci's category of *hegemony* and the necessity for organic intellectuals as useful to developing Black theology as revolutionary praxis.[29]

29. Cornel West, *Prophesy Deliverance! An Afro-American Revolutionary Christianity* (Philadelphia: Westminster, 1982), 119.

Gramsci's category of *hegemony* helps explain how the oppressed masses in a society give their consent to be exploited by the dominant group, through their social life and the "prestige which the dominant group enjoys because of its position and function in the world of production."[30] Traditional intellectuals and ecclesiastics prop up the state, help legitimize the status quo, and are instrumental in convincing the masses to accept their status and economic exploitation. West's critique of the absence of class analysis within Black theology, coupled with William Jones's contention that Black theology is riddled with the residue of the oppressor's worldview in its inability to present a proper theodicy to explain Black suffering, suggests that Black theologians (and most Black pastors), even in their vehement opposition to white theology, are traditional intellectuals bound to the state and the status quo either by denominational allegiances or tenure expectations and/or professional academic commitments. In being bound to the state, Black theology has to conform to the universal imperatives of state-sanctioned theology—American or Western forms of Christianity. The requirement that Christian theology be universal, a tenet of white epistemological hubris, obscures the particular focus on Blacks' struggle to eradicate double-consciousness and actually diminishes the urgency of liberation or spiritual, social, and political transformation particular to the experiences of Black people.

Organic intellectuals, however, are able to function in a way that allows them to develop praxis-oriented theories or theologies that avoid the ideological limitations and disciplinary gatekeeping with which traditional intellectuals must contend. Organic intellectuals, according to Gramsci, emerge within a social class or group and are able to direct the thought of the

---

30. Antonio Gramsci, *Prison Notebooks*, volume 1 (New York: Columbia University Press, 1992), 12.

group and to develop and participate in praxis-related solutions based on the needs, concerns, and problems of that group.[31] The organic intellectual is able to formulate new knowledge (i.e., knowledge not considered knowledge by the status quo, or "subjugated knowledge") and to establish a new standard for what is possible by foregrounding the actual problems intrinsic to the group itself and not some concern sanctioned by tradition or the state. Black theology has been unable to establish itself as independent in this way and thus continues to suffer from the double-consciousness it claims to combat or resist.

Both Cleage and Tetteh, however, in their respective contexts (African American and West African) are organic intellectuals who each develop African-centered theologies of spatial healing and recovery in their efforts to foreground the problem of double-consciousness or second-sight in African-descended people. Because they prioritize the need to ameliorate and overcome Black/African self-hatred or the acceptance of Black inferiority, in order to create a church community that can be a vanguard for a liberation struggle or a transforming community, they are not preoccupied with the white or imperial gaze, nor do they seek white academic or denominational validation or legitimation from entities outside the communities they lead. As pastor theologians, they each established church communities/institutions independent of denominational affiliation, yet neither is a professional academic (Tetteh often proclaims forthrightly that he does not even have a college degree). As such, they represent true organic intellection, which frees them to create theologies guided by the pragmatic goal of liberation, or spiritual, social, and political transformation.

Cleage was initially associated with the Congregational and then the United Church of Christ denominations; however, in

---

31. Gramsci, *Prison Notebooks*, 1:12.

1967 he founded the Shrine of the Black Madonna of the Pan African Orthodox Christian Church as an independent Protestant denomination. Responding to the cry for Black Power and Black self-determination by a younger generation of Black Power advocates who had grown weary with the nonviolent, integrationist approach of Martin Luther King Jr. in late-1960s America, Cleage wrote and established the Black Christian Nationalist Manifesto. In it, he states that the Black church must remake itself and no longer function as an instrument in pursuit of white respectability and otherworldly salvation if it is to serve as a viable instrument of Black liberation. Cleage exhorts,

> The black church must free the minds of Black people from psychological "identification" with a white society which seeks in every way to destroy them. Black people who dream of integration perpetuate the mechanism of their enslavement. They have been programmed to destroy themselves. The Black church must fight to free the black man's mind so that he can fight to restructure or destroy the institutions which perpetuate his enslavement.[32]

Cleage argues that the Black church helped perpetuate the myth of Black inferiority in its acceptance of a white image of Jesus Christ and a white male God. He accused the Black church, and the dominant white American culture as a whole, of creating a slave culture for Blacks that engaged in a process of "niggerizing" Black people in America. This "niggerization process" is designed to convince Black people of their innate inferiority, and theology, especially Christology, is the servant of this process.

32. Albert B. Cleage Jr., Unpublished sermon.

> Until black Christians are ready to challenge this lie [a white Christ], they have not freed themselves from their spiritual bondage to the white man nor established in their minds their right to first class citizenship in Christ's kingdom on earth. Black people cannot build dignity on their knees worshipping a white Christ. We must put down this white Jesus which the white man gave us in slavery and which has been tearing us to pieces.[33]

Cleage's priority was to convince Black people of their self-worth by rejecting the dream of integration within white society but instead becoming an independent, self-determining people. His primary concern was eradicating double-consciousness, and his Black Christian Nationalist theology reflects that.

Cleage is often misunderstood as being fixated on race and merely inverting the racial hierarchy so that Black people have more power than white people. Such misunderstanding, however, derives from an inability to delineate the early Cleage from the later Cleage, especially since the later Cleage never published his revised theology in any formal way and still relied on the racial rhetoric popular at the time. While the early Cleage's declaration that Black people are God's chosen people conveys an acceptance of racial essentialism, and while the early Cleage did present Christianity as a nationalistic religion for Black people (he argued that the original Hebrews were racially Black), the later Cleage evolved beyond a theology and interpretation of the gospel predicated solely on the racial dynamics particular to the history of Black and white relations in America. To remain in this reactionary space would be to limit God to a "slice of time." Cleage's evolution was propelled by his insistence that the telos of

---

33. Albert B. Cleage Jr., "An Introduction to Black Christian Nationalism" (unpublished essay), 2.

Black liberation ultimately requires a reckoning with and a reclamation of Black people's African heritage and African systems
of knowledge. His efforts to reconnect Black people with traditional African spirituality and ways of knowing led him to theologically engage African mysticism as the basis for overcoming
racist social conditioning in America. I quote him at length here.

> You find in today's world Communalism among Black
> people is almost as rare as it is among white people.
> Everybody is living for himself. To do what he can for
> himself, to get what he can for himself. And, in all
> his relationships with other people he is exploited. So,
> Black people are doing the same thing that they see
> white people doing all around them, because we have
> come to the conclusion that whatever the white man
> does is right, because he's got power. He controls the
> institutions. He controls society. So, we try to be like
> him and in trying to be like him we shut off areas and
> avenues of knowledge and information which Black
> people had thousands of years ago, which Black people
> had four hundred years ago. Three hundred years ago,
> which today we do not pay attention to because we are
> ashamed to have kinds of information, intuitive knowl-
> edge the white man has not given us. We are ashamed
> of information which we secure for ourselves, which
> God gives us, rather than what we secure from reading
> a book which a white man has written.[34]

Cleage eventually arrives at a conception of God as cosmic
energy and creative intelligence, or a pantheistic view of the one-

---

34. Albert B. Cleage Jr., "Beyond Rational Consciousness, Part 2"
(unpublished sermon).

ness of God, that makes his theology no longer parochial or racially exclusive and derives from, although is not equivalent to, a precolonial, pre-Western, African mystical view. It should also be noted that his revised conception of God is responsive to Jones's critique of Cleage's original claim of Blacks' *chosenness* and his early embrace of a Black God, even though Jones mischaracterizes Cleage's theodicy as one of deserved punishment for Black people. Cleage's turn to African theism allows him to transcend the theological restrictions and intellectual parochialisms of the Black God. Theological interest in the African religious heritage leads him to a conception of God that resonates with the African independent church pastor/theologian Ishmael Tetteh, whose point of departure is similarly the urgency of eradicating double-consciousness in African people. Their similar theologies, derived from their respective contexts, convey a transcontextual, or even Pan-African, consciousness linked by their shared conception of God. In this way, they bridge the spatial distance between African Americans and West Africans. They each Africanize the Westernized spaces around them.

Brother Tetteh, like Cleage, is motivated by the problem of double-consciousness in his context of Ghana, West Africa. To him, West Africans view themselves and their culture through an imperial gaze, and religion is the primary mechanism through which this is accomplished. He notes that "the African is systematically encouraged to look down upon her culture. Today, the tool being used to mentally destroy the African culture is religion.… Catholic and Protestant missionaries have done their worst onslaught on African cultural practices.… The war on African culture is currently being propagated through the Pentecostal and Charismatic ministries."[35] While Tetteh

---

35. Ishmael N. O. Tetteh, *The Inspired African Mystical Gospel*, volume 1 (Accra, Ghana: Etherean Mission Publishing, 2001), 24.

uses racial categories at times to describe the colonizer/colonized binary, he maintains that the process of "niggerization" fundamentally derives from the denigration and disparagement of traditional African religious cultures, or the way Western perceptions of the African are based on what Engelbert Mveng refers to as "the anthropological poverty of the African person."[36] Tetteh describes African anthropological impoverishment and, more specifically, double-consciousness this way:

> It is the African who must awaken to his values. This is where the problem emanates. We seem to have been set like puppets thinking according to a set pattern designed by some other race for us. Colonise the mind of a man and you have got a willing slave forever. A look at the African continent presents nothing but economic and social deprivation. In spite of our great universities producing many learned men, it seems the ability for Africans to think right for themselves is yet to come. Have you wondered why our learned men do not thrive well on our own soils, yet when they travel to the white man's land they perform miracles? The answer is simple; the thinking pattern of the African is tuned to foreign cultures and can only function properly in the foreign countries.[37]

Here Tetteh is describing how imperialism functions as a field of knowledge, specifically how colonial education works to position Western knowledge and ways of understanding as superior to African knowledge production. Africa's spiritual and

---

36. Engelbert Mveng, "Third World Theology—What Theology? What Third World?," in *The Irruption of the Third World: Challenge to Theology,* ed. Virginia Fabella and Sergio Torres (Maryknoll, NY: Orbis Books, 1983), 220.

37. Tetteh, *Inspired African Mystical Gospel,* 27.

cultural impoverishment is perpetuated by the loss of human resources through colonial education, even when those schools and universities are run and controlled by Africans. Tetteh calls for African religious and cultural renewal but not a return to an unattainable, "pristine" precolonial past. He accepts and embraces the presence of Christianity and the church but calls for a distinctly African interpretation of the religion, or an African church, that can interpret the gospel of Jesus, or Yeshua, in a way consistent with the norms and values of African culture. "What we have today in Africa, and Ghana for that matter, is not the Yeshua Jew culture-based Christianity; it is the Western-based Christianity. To prefer another culture to yours under the guise of religion is to castrate the good of God's presence in yourself. That certainly constitutes spiritual suicide."[38]

What is clear is that both Cleage and Tetteh identify internalized acceptance of Black and African inferiority, or second-sight, as the most important challenge facing churches comprising African-descended peoples. My assertion is that both attempt to address this through radical transformation of their theologies, away from Western Christian formulations or methodological imperatives, by embracing African mysticism or what I call a turn toward an Africana theological methodology. We can examine the methodology through explication and analysis of their respective doctrines of God, the symbol that connects their agendas, which rejects an anthropomorphic conception and limiting categories like monotheism and polytheism in favor of the idea of God as the creative power, intelligence, and energy that subsumes the universe. They both embrace a spatial conception of God (i.e., God is the energy and power in us and all around us) that rejects the conventional Western God believed to possess human-like agency. Yet it is also not a rigid

---

38. Mveng, "Third World Theology," 30.

adherence to the pre-colonial African God and gods. Once African mysticism is embraced as a source for developing theology and a resource for resolving double-consciousness, these theologians, in their different, Pan-African contexts, develop identical conceptions of God unbeknownst to each other. In so doing, they pivot away from preoccupation with the white or imperial gaze and rediscover what indigenous African thought has to contribute to postmodern constructions of knowledge.

Similar to the suggestion by some ecotheologians, anthropomorphic symbolization is being jettisoned in this model. While it might serve the practical function of helping human beings relate to divinity, such symbolization is inadequate because human forms are limited and bound by configurations of space and time. God as creative power, energy, and intelligence presents a God-symbol that is infinitely spatial. This means that God can be accessed in any and all spaces, those we presently occupy and those untouched by humans. This God is the God of every present moment, not a God we have to scour the past for to see "his" work. Problematically, the anthropomorphic model always leaves us with more questions. For example, how can a God in the form of a human being (classical theism) occupy space in two places at once? How can God see, optically, all 7.7 billion people on the planet simultaneously? How can God hear billions or even hundreds of millions of prayers at the same time? Human beings are limited, yet God, by definition, is unlimited. So anthropomorphic characterizations or symbols of God are flawed because they inevitably lead to a static conception of divinity assigning human-like agency when those symbols inevitably become literal and entrenched in our psyches. Terms such as *energy, power, intelligence*, and *spirit*, however, are symbols that effectively describe a more amorphous and intangible reality consistent with the African mystical view of God. These categories are preferred because they lead us to describe reality and understand the task of religion and religious practices in new ways. This God-symbol helps to overcome the false perception of reality as bifurcated, which is what double-consciousness depends on for its existence. Racial categories emanate from a Eurocentric classification of difference. African cosmology provides useful categories and a doctrine of God to help vitiate the devastating impact of second-sight. It merges the twoness into a single, authentic, self-consciousness or awareness that understands the unity of all existence.

Tetteh speaks of the indwelling presence of God in us, what Cleage calls the God incarnate. "God is the Intelligent energy that constitutes all of life and that everyone is an expression of. God cannot be Omnipresent without being present in everyone. Since God is Omnipotent and Omnipresent, His/Her greatness permeates all life."[39] The radical immanence of God is key to both theologies because this indwelling spirit and power provide the necessary energy to struggle for transformation. Tetteh goes on to describe God this way:

> The creator is not separate from creation. The African, predominantly a farmer and noticing that without the earth, water, sunlight and air, the seed will not grow concludes that the one life that God is, is revealed as these four elements and more. Veneration to the Deity is sometimes channeled through these four elements. The river god, the sun god, the earth god and the god of air are all aspects of the one presence of God.[40]

Here Tetteh describes how the elements of nature constitute a visible representation of the power source that is God. River god,

39. Emmanuel Yartekwei Amugi Lartey, *Postcolonializing God: New Perspectives on Pastoral and Practical Theology* (London: SCM Press, 2013), 73.
40. Tetteh, *Inspired African Mystical Gospel*, 41.

sun god, and earth god are symbols that point to the energy that undergirds and enables each.

Cleage talks about God in various sermons using a similar vocabulary when he declares,

> God is cosmic energy and creative intelligence out of which all things were created. There's no way God can be a man off someplace, a big man … there's no way. Everything that exists is in a web of energy, cosmic energy and creative intelligence. God continues to be the energy field in which all the forces of nature are united. That's very different from a man sitting off someplace. All the forces of nature are united in one single energy field.[41]

This alternative conception of God is not merely a semantic change but radically subverts and alters the task of religion itself, away from a quietist position to empowering the practitioner to seek positive political and social transformation of their environment. This African conception of God offers a counter-hegemonic approach that religion can use to bring about radical spiritual, social, and political transformation. Cleage insisted we view God as a power source that could be tapped into to bring about social change within Black communities.

> In a sense you are conscious of the unified cosmic energy field in which you live and move and have your being. You are conscious of an inner life force and experiences that are beyond comprehension. If you think about them, a vast and invisible network of energy paths unite all things. We could think of it as energy paths, and energy paths everywhere you walk; you are

---

41. Albert B. Cleage Jr., "God Is Power" (unpublished sermon).

walking through energy fields. Energy fields are moving through you. But you have to somehow be able to
plug into the energy field for it to become meaningful
to you.… The possibilities of plugging into whole layers
of existence of understanding is possible but you never
understand it. You never become aware of it. The vast
invisible network of energy paths unites all things. We
are in touch with God at all times if we choose to plug
in. We are in touch with each other at all times if we
choose to plug in (1982).[42]

Plugging in to God as a mechanism for raising one's consciousness in order to engage in social transformation conveys
a conjurational spirituality. It speaks to God's immediate avail-
ability in the present spaces we occupy. The notion that we can
plug into God also reveals Cleage's alternative answer to what
Jones uncovers as the fundamental flaw within Black theology.
Jones's critique exposes his worry that Black theology cannot do
what it claims. He is concerned that Black theology is a theology of liberation only rhetorically, and is, in fact, still bound to
the oppressor's theology because it accepts a theodicy that leads
the Black Christian to quietism. *Quietism* is an orientation in
which one accepts suffering as willed by God. Jones contends
that, by relying on traditional theodicies, such as the redemptive
suffering theodicy, Black theology ultimately places the onus on
God to bring about liberation for Black people and not on Black
people themselves.

Pinn has long argued that theodicy is an attempt to justify
God's existence and goodness at the expense of the integrity of
human beings. In the case of Black suffering, this means that
Black people must accept that "religion must encourage believers

42. Cleage, "God Is Power."

to surrender something. They must surrender certain modalities of experience, certain ways of knowing, and grant authority to an unproven but assumed to be concerned God."[43] For Pinn, Black Christians are forced to concede that either "God endorses evil, does not exist, or that there must be some merit in suffering."[44] He criticizes Black theology for choosing the latter and instead endorses the claim that God does not exist and human beings are functionally ultimate. But it seems that these are not the only options. Pinn's argument depends on a God-symbol that presumably expresses agency the same way humans do. Thus, human beings are expected to believe that faithfulness to God means giving up, or turning over, agency to a transcendent God as a test of obedience to God's will. But if God is the power source that we plug into, then, like spirit and breath, God works in concert with our agency. God enables our agency. This God does not express a divine will at all but is an amoral, neutral force. Consequently, God is not a white racist, God does not require our suffering, nor is God on the side of the oppressed.

In turning toward an African mystical conception of God, both Cleage and Tetteh create theologies that address Jones's most salient critique of the shortcomings of Black theology, double-consciousness, and posit a God-symbol that speaks to the dual demands for racial justice and ecological recovery. If God is the energy, intelligence, and power existing within us and all around us, and not a super divine being, transcendent, separate, and distinct, then accessing and channeling or plugging into the energy and power of God is the fundamental task of religion. Demonstrating to practitioners how to enhance one's connection to that energy is an act of worship. The choice

43. Anthony Pinn, "On the Question at the End of Theodicy," *Religions* 8 (December 2017): 2.

44. Pinn, "On the Question at the End," 2.

to then use that energy collaboratively to fight oppression and/ or restore balance and harmony to the ecosphere is a decision humans make without the assistance of God. Doing this transforms the act of worship and the Christian religious experience. No longer is worship an act of appeasing or placating a vengeful and temperamental being who grants favor only to those who follow a list of enigmatic rules or succeed in pacifying or satiating a divine thirst for justice. Prayer is no longer about convincing the deity that we are worthy of divine attention and special treatment, in spite of the often stated claim that one does not merit grace. Worship is not about vying for divine attention and proving our worthiness to a whimsical God.

The focus of the worship experience shifts from the vertical to the horizontal, a spatial conception. Emphasis is placed on the energy, power, and spirit generated with other people who occupy the same space(s)—energy that has the power to heal, generate love or hate, and provide necessary insight to empower people to work in their own best interest. God is the activating power leading one to effectively struggle for liberation. Cleage pointedly notes how a pantheistic conception of God alters the church worship experience and clarifies the task and nature of the church in the world today.

> Much of the confusion about the nature of the church stems from our differing conceptions of God. The church as "transforming community" mediates the power of God. The church *acts for God in the world*. Those things which we have come to expect from God, comfort, solace, healing, security, guidance, help, forgiveness, strength, understanding, purpose, and an "after life," must be delivered by the communal fellowship of the church through which God has elected to act because we are "the chosen," and have established

a covenant relationship. God as cosmic energy and creative intelligence has no other "body" to house the infinite power of the "Unified Field" through which all possibilities are open to the church.[45]

For Cleage, the *communal fellowship* is the vehicle through which God's will is realized in the world. These people are the *chosen* only insofar as they have come to understand how God power actually works in the world. They have chosen the appropriate God-symbol. But notice that Cleage's use of *chosen* here makes no reference to racial categories. Black people are not chosen, or special, because of their blackness or because of their oppressed existence. In fact, most Black Christians continue to accept the God of classical theism and are thus unable to be *the body* of God in the world. By incorporating this doctrine of God within his theology, Cleage teaches of the oneness of existence, and racial categories are exposed as fictions created for the sole purpose of perpetuating white supremacy. While ending racial oppression and establishing Black self-determination are still his task, Cleage abandons the racial essentialist position that this project can be accomplished only by people of a specific hue or physical appearance. If God power is accessible to any group of individuals open to receiving such power, then no particular cultural perspective or religion has a monopoly on or exclusive access to divine truth. This conception of God points toward a pluralistic, even scientific understanding of religious faith and religious practice. Cleage conveys the point here in a way similar to Tetteh:

> Little church, big church, whatever it is, if it is a group of Christians who are committed to God, who accept Jesus, the revelation of Jesus as one way of finding God,

45. Cleage, "Beyond Rational Consciousness."

and we do not hold that Jesus is the only method that people have for finding a relationship with God. All of the religions of the world stem from Africa. Black people talked with God, knew God, had a relationship with God, long before Jesus.… But Christianity is certainly one of the basic ways that people can find the meaning of God, because God was incarnate in Jesus. Not in a special sense, but incarnate in Jesus as God can be incarnate in anyone of you. It means God possessed him. He had an experience of God.[46]

The idea that God possessed Jesus in a way that God can possess anyone illustrates that the task of religion is to increase one's awareness of and access to God power. Jesus is not unique, nor should we constantly dwell on his acts and past experiences alone. God power is accessible in any moment in any space by any body, human and otherwise. We must now consider the ramifications of this theology for traditional Christian symbols like the Bible and the cross.

Conclusion

I call Cleage and Tetteh *organic intellectuals* because they develop creative theologies derived from their racial/ethnic, working-class context and consciousness. Because they are not tied to institutions, academic or ecclesiastical, representing the state and upholding the status quo, they are able to create theologies attentive to the concerns that emerge from within their group and not to the perceptions imposed on them from those without, the psychological legacy of second-sight. I argue that the problem each is determined to resolve or eradicate is double-

46. Cleage, "Beyond Rational Consciousness."

consciousness. Heretofore, Black theology has been unable to fully address the malady of double-consciousness because it is itself preoccupied with the white or imperial gaze. Ontological blackness, the theodicy of redemptive suffering, and the claim that God is on the side of the oppressed all evince a fetishism of revelation and the biblical God-symbol. Even ecotheology, which goes further than other contemporary theologies in revising its God-symbol, is still apologetic and not fully committed to non-agential God-symbols.

Cleage and Tetteh, however, expand the sources for doing Christian theology to include African mysticism. In so doing, they avoid traps of both racial reification and the fetishism of the revelation of Jesus Christ. Their understanding of God as creative energy, power, and intelligence transforms the task of religion away from the trap of theodicy and the passivity of quietism to a vehicle or mechanism that stimulates and inspires action and the energy necessary for social, political, and spiritual transformation. It prioritizes the goal of human, particularly Black/African, liberation and eschews the traditional requirement that theology engage in Christian apologetics. What emerges is a God that is neither a white racist nor a being on the side of the oppressed. What emerges is a theology of spatial healing and recovery utilizing the African epistemological modality of *elasticity,* which incorporates, instead of excluding, pragmatic ideas and concepts from outside its system to advance the empowerment of the individual and/or group.

Finally, by comparing these two theologians, one African American and one West African, I offer a model for engaging in transcontextual discourse and cultivating a Pan-African consciousness that can begin to heal the devastating effect of racialization and African cultural denigration brought about by the hegemonic religion and cultures of the white, Christian West.

Focus on the transcontext provides a means for Black theology to avoid the charge of being theologically parochial and racially exclusive. It traverses the spatial terrain and reconnects African-descended people who have been geographically dislocated and spatially alienated. This approach focuses attention on what African people on the continent and throughout the diaspora have in common—the need to finally eradicate the Black/African inferiority complex and its preoccupation with the white gaze. Cleage and Tetteh provide a theology neither exclusively Christian nor traditionally African but Pan-African, Africana, a creolized, hybrid, and pragmatic theology whose central concerns are spiritual, social, and political transformation and ecological healing and recovery.

4

Black Suffering and the Urgency for New Theological Symbols

Constructing Christian theology in a way that prioritizes spatial configurations over temporal ones invites us to consider new possibilities for theological categories, symbols, and biblical hermeneutics that move us away from both a reification of the past and the false universalization of religion, specifically Christianity, especially as represented in the category "Word of God." I argue that the essence of white epistemological hubris is the projection of a culturally specific, sociohistorically located understanding of truth onto all people, but especially onto oppressed African-descended peoples, and that it manifests itself in a vicious individualism. White hubris, the germ seed of whiteness, infects Christian theologizing, including biblical hermeneutics. Movement away from the temporally oriented to the spatially oriented shifts the epistemological ground upon which we approach traditional theological categories and invites us not only to interpret the Bible subversively but to expand consideration of what counts as acceptable "sources" for doing theology.

I stated that Black theology must expand its sources beyond those deemed acceptable by traditional Western theology. In an earlier work, I posited the African notion of ancestor as a category of meaning offering a more liberatory conception of theological anthropology, or the doctrine of the human being, than the Western Christian conception of the human being tied to ontological sin. The notion of ancestor also offers a renunciation of the false universalism implicit in the claim that Jesus is the exclusive savior and sole historical, and indeed special, revelation. Now I will expand on and develop the ancestors as a theological category that helps us to honor the sanctity of the ground, the land/Earth we inhabit, and to reframe religion as culturally particular, contextual, and pragmatically efficacious in resistance to racial oppression and also useful in the restoration of balance and harmony to the Earth. The ancestors call out to us to preserve the land, to restore the spaces in which they continue to reside, to reimagine Black identity formation, and to rethink redemption, struggle, salvation, and liberation in light of the constancy of Black suffering, antiblack violence, and Black social death.

In this chapter, I attempt to demonstrate that Black Christians' and Black theology's continuous reliance on the presumed redemptive capacities of the cross and the Bible as symbols of salvation work to support the claims of Afropessimism that Blackness equates to slaveness and is marked by *social death.* Orlando Patterson was the first to coin the term *social death,* by which he meant that enslaved Africans are not subjects but mere objects of history who have no existence outside that of the master.[1] This term is crucial for understanding the formation of white identity as well since the slave master's social status is maintained by virtue of his complete domination and control of the enslaved. Afropessimism's claim is that black social death continued long after chattel slavery as an institution ended, extending even into

---

1. Orlando Patterson, "Authority, Alienation, and Social Death," in *African-American Religious Thought: An Anthology,* ed. Cornel West and Eddie S. Glaude Jr. (Louisville: Westminster John Knox Press, 2003).

the present moment. Black Christians have not freed themselves from the specter of social death, in part because they continue to interpret Christian symbols, specifically the cross and the Bible, through the lens of whiteness and in so doing evince the double-consciousness discussed in an earlier chapter.

Anthony Pinn argues that Afropessimism challenges African American religious thought's "organizing principles and disrupts its metaphysical assumptions making possible its existential claims."[2] I call for a rejection of the cross as a central Christian symbol, to be replaced by the category "ancestor," and then demand that we engage in biblical hermeneutics (if we are to engage in biblical hermeneutics) in a way that unashamedly serves the interests of oppressed African-descended people. In other words, Black people should affirm their own cultural bias in interpreting scripture and should interpret scripture through the lens of "struggle," if the text is to be used as a source at all.

The Cross and Black Social Death

Christina Sharpe argues that Black existence in America, despite the illusion of racial progress, continues to be defined by and instantiated within the aftermath of slavery or, more accurately, *in the wake* of slavery. By this she means that slavery persists in the American consciousness as a continuous *unresolved unfolding*.[3] Here she draws upon Frank Wilderson's Afropessimist claim that "Blacks are not Human subjects, but are instead structurally inert props, implements for the execution of White and non-Black fantasies and sadomasochistic

2. Anthony Pinn, "What Can Be Said? African American Religious Thought, Afro-Pessimism, and the Question of Hope," *Black Theology: An International Journal* 18:2 (2020), 151.

3. Christina Sharpe, *In the Wake: On Blackness and Being* (Durham, NC: Duke University Press, 2016), 14.

pleasures."[4] According to Wilderson, it is not just white people who extract their humanity from their oppositional relationship to Black people (in the sense that white equals human) but also other non-Black people. He argues that the claims of universal humanity manifest a contradiction, "a contradiction that manifests whenever one looks seriously at the structure of Black suffering in comparison to the presumed universal structure of all sentient beings."[5] Black suffering in America, he argues, is of a scale that arguably makes redress or reparation untenable, even inconceivable. Thus, "A Black radical agenda is terrifying to most people on the Left—think Bernie Sanders—because it emanates from a condition of suffering for which there is no imaginable strategy for redress—no narrative of social, political, or national redemption."[6]

On this point, Christianity has been particularly derelict and has, in fact, failed Black people, in part because theological categories like redemption, sin, and salvation offer no redress to the specter of Black social death. These categories fail, in part, because they emerge from a tradition and language subsumed in a feigned universality, which makes such terms inevitably abstract and disconnected from lived Black experience. Even Black theology at times fails Black people to the extent that it also conforms to the accepted imperative toward universality and in so doing creates categories that too often obfuscate Blackness in its quotidian forms. As a result, Black people lack a proper language or discourse, theological, philosophical, or otherwise, a proper vocabulary that can speak to "our abjection from the realm of humanity."[7] It is in this lacuna or gap

4. Frank B. Wilderson III, *Afropessimism* (New York: Liveright, 2020), 15.

5. Wilderson, *Afropessimism*, 15.

6. Wilderson, *Afropessimism*, 15.

7. Wilderson, *Afropessimism*, 14.

that Afropessimism positions itself. As a metatheory, it questions the adequacy of Black strands of thought that have their theoretical grounding in the assumptions of Western academia and Western rationalism. Sharpe's term *wake,* as in the wake of the slave ship, helps to frame the persistence and resiliency of vicious antiblackness despite the long Black struggle to resist and overcome it. Martin Luther King Jr.'s message that we shall overcome and his insistence that the "moral arc of the universe is long but it bends toward justice" notwithstanding, what continues unabated in America is the constancy of antiblack violence and Black social death.

Since slavery, in the *afterlife of property*, Black people have been subjected to ritual spectacle lynching, vicious land dispossession, and most recently wanton killing and murder at the hands of law enforcement officers, whose stated job description is to protect and serve, or entitled vigilantes posing as law enforcement. In this sense, the lynching of Sam Hose in Coweta County, Georgia, in 1899 is no different than the murder of George Floyd in Minneapolis, Minnesota, in the summer of 2020. The lynching of Mary Turner in Georgia in 1918, in which she was hanged, doused with gasoline, set on fire, and riddled with hundreds of bullets for merely publically calling the whites who murdered her husband to a legal accounting, is a slight difference in degree but not in kind from the 2020 police shooting murder of Breonna Taylor in Louisville, Kentucky—given the level of overkill, the depravity of whiteness, and the degree to which Black bodies continue to be objectified, reduced to the *afterlife of property*, and too often killed. For Sharpe, this suggests that "living in the wake means living in and with terror in that in much of what passes for public discourse *about* terror we, Black people, become the *carriers* of terror, terror's embodiment, and not the primary objects of terror's multiple enactments; the ground of terror's possibility globally."[8] She concludes with the imperative, "I want *In the Wake* to declare that we are Black peoples in the wake with no state or nation to protect us, with no citizenship bound to be respected, and to position us in the modalities of Black life lived in, as, under, despite Black death; to think and be and act from there."[9] Such an imperative challenges the stated goals and prerogatives of Black theology as an American theology of liberation and demands a creative reimagining of theology as a system of thought.

How might Black people capitalize on, or embrace, the status of no-citizen to reimagine citizenship in global terms, in Earthly terms, in ways that reconstitute the spatial plane beyond the province of the North American land mass? How might we tap into our African heritage, our transatlantic heritage, to draw out categories that address both the problem of Black social death and the urgent need to restore the Earth? The ancestor as a category offers the potential to fill a void and offer a way to reclaim Black personhood, overcome social death, and restore Black spaces as we exist *in the wake.*

James Cone's *The Cross and the Lynching Tree* elucidates the cross as a Christian symbol and explains it in a way that captures Sharpe's claim that Black people are *carriers of terror and are terror's embodiment.* What he does most importantly is expose the white ignorance that lies at the heart of white theology by pointing out the failure of white theologians, for example, Reinhold Niebuhr, to see the obvious theological connection between the execution of Jesus, the Christ, by way of crucifixion and the lynching from trees, the hanging deaths, of thousands of Black men, women, and children, mostly in the ninety-year period that marked the end of Reconstruction in the South to the rise

8. Sharpe, *In the Wake*, 15.
9. Sharpe, *In the Wake*, 22.

of the civil rights movement in America in the mid-twentieth century. For Cone, the correlation between the cross and the lynching tree reveals both the horror and the brutality of the cross, rejecting its romanticism, and simultaneously renders sacred the Black bodies unjustly hanged from trees, brutalized, and desecrated by white Christians during this period in American history.

Ultimately, Cone's text is a meditation and reflection on the cross as perhaps the most powerful and resonant Christian symbol for Black Americans. For him, it is the cross that is open to interpretation. "The cross can heal and hurt; it can be empowering and liberating but also enslaving and oppressive. There is no one way in which the cross can be interpreted."[10] Here Cone continues the Black Christian tradition of taking religious symbols introduced to Black Christians by white Christians and offering a radically different interpretation of that symbol in order to purify and justify it. As with the religion of Christianity itself, the point is that the flaw lies not with the symbol itself but with traditional white interpretations of it. Cone states outright that, while the cross was brandished as a religious symbol to terrorize (e.g., the Ku Klux Klan's burning cross), for Black people it symbolized divine power, "God overcoming the power of sin and death." He argues that, during the period of lynching, Black people identified with the innocence and undeserved nature of Jesus's suffering because it mirrored their own suffering. As a powerless minority in a brutishly, antiblack society, Black Christians gravitated to the idea that divine glory could be attained through innocent, redemptive suffering. On this point, Cone goes so far as to claim that "the final word about Black life is not death on the lynching tree but redemption in

---

10. James H. Cone, *The Cross and the Lynching Tree* (Maryknoll, NY: Orbis Books, 2011), xix.

the cross … but the cross speaks to oppressed people in ways that Jesus's life, teachings, and even his resurrection do not."[11] The latter point warrants further interrogation, especially in light of Cone's criticism of the racist blind spots in the theology of Reinhold Niebuhr.

I question whether the cross is overdetermined in Cone's theology, and in Black Christianity generally, in a way that reveals a dearth of effective religious symbols in Black Christianity and exposes a lack of creativity in the Black theological imagination. Furthermore, a question can be asked if an overreliance on the cross does harm by instantiating the acceptability of Black suffering in the consciousness of Black, non-Black, and white people, thus preserving and failing to adequately critique or dismantle white domination and white power's legitimacy.

Cone discusses Niebuhr in depth and posits him as a white theologian most known for making the cross central to his theology. Niebuhr argues that the cross signifies the *transvaluation of values*[12] and how God's transcendent love is hidden in Jesus's suffering. The cross is supposed to teach us that there is power in weakness and that the divine honors "man's" lowliness over his pride. Here Niebuhr is making a theological claim that he would posit as universally applicable since pride, for him, is the original sin. For Niebuhr, the atoning death of Jesus on the cross is God's response to human sin. According to him, "It is an actual fact that human life, which is always threatened and periodically engulfed by the evil that human sin creates, is also marvelously redeemed by the transmutation of evil [the cross] into good [the resurrection]. This transmutation is not a human but a divine possibility. No man can, by taking thought, turn

11. Cone, *Cross and the Lynching Tree*, 26.
12. Reinhold Niebuhr, *Beyond Tragedy: Essays on the Christian Interpretation of Tragedy* (New York: Charles Scribner's Sons, 1937), 197.

evil into good."[13] The cross teaches human beings not to be lured into a false optimism by any perceived good or pushed into a deep despair by any horrible tragedy. This forms the basis for Niebuhr's Christian realism.

Yet, when it came time to apply his theology of the cross to a specific episode of racial conflict and division in 1950s and 1960s America, Niebuhr revealed his cultural and racial bias on behalf of whiteness. Niebuhr was slow to criticize Southern whites, many of whom were violently opposed to desegregation of American schools, and he clearly demonstrated more sympathy for white people reluctant to integrate, than with oppressed Black people eager to gain freedom and equality. Niebuhr's posture evinces white epistemological hubris, because his embrace of pride as a manifestation of universal, ontological sin blinds him to the possibility that pride as ultimate, foundational sin might not be universal but specific to a particular cultural orientation. His reading of the tragedy and triumph of the cross as universal corrective to the sin of pride is flawed. Niebuhr's problem is the arrogant assumption that he can speak both for white people and Black people in America while seemingly being oblivious to his own racial positionality, his white privilege. Cone correctly criticizes him but fails to repudiate the false universalism implicit in his own interpretation of the cross or to interrogate the extent to which his view of the cross as the central Christian symbol provides shelter and even protection for white authority to promote slow incremental racial change and inclusion. From his perch of white authority, Niebuhr fails, in his theology of the cross, to prioritize or render preference to Black suffering; thus Black suffering remains obscured as a type of universal suffering no different from white suffering (for

13. Niebuhr, *Beyond Tragedy*, 20.

example, suffering derived from the prospect of white children having to attend school with Black children).

Cone rightly accuses Niebuhr of manifesting an empathy deficit as regards his inability to identify with the suffering of Black people. The question is whether Black Christians' embrace of this same symbol also contributes to that empathy deficit. Does Cone's claim that the cross *speaks to oppressed people in ways that Jesus's life, teachings, and even his resurrection do not* suggest an overreliance on the cross as constitutive of Black existence, leading to a glorification of Black suffering and Black people's ability to endure suffering, thus helping to rationalize white ignorance and propel even further the empathy gap between whites and Blacks? How well has the cross served Black Christians beyond helping them endure racial suffering? Has it ever actually functioned as a symbol of liberation? It seems that, even as Cone rejects Martin Luther King Jr.'s understanding of redemptive suffering and its conflation with his philosophy of nonviolence and *agape* love for one's oppressor, Cone still affirms and promotes the redemptive power of Jesus's suffering and death. He does not reject the Niebuhrian claim that God transmutes evil (suffering) into good (redemption). Against the backdrop of the lynching tree, the notion of redemptive suffering even further raises the question William Jones asked: Where is the redemption event for Black people that justifies the suffering and the constancy of Black social death? What is the event that proves that the suffering was in fact redemptive? How has Black Christian belief in the cross, from the period of slavery through the nadir of racist lynchings to the present, appreciably changed the condition of violent antiblackness in America? Can we conclude that acceptance of this theology of the cross actually works in furtherance of Black social death? Does Black Christian acceptance of this symbol not work to legitimize, even render mundane, Black social death?

Black theology and mainstream Black church theology's inability to sufficiently answer these questions creates a maddening silence, resulting in a vacuum filled by Afropessimism. There has not been, nor will there ever be, a redemptive event if, as Wilderson argues, "Blackness is coterminous with Slaveness. Blackness is social death. Blackness as a paradigmatic position … cannot be disimbricated from slavery," in large part because white "humanity" depends on this conception of Blackness for its life.[14] Whiteness sucks the life and the humanity out of Blackness, reducing it to property. This happens epistemologically when we equate white Western thought and perspectives with objectivity and with that which is universally efficacious. The inability to dislodge whiteness and objectivity relegates Blackness, also Africanness, to an inferior tier, to the realm of the subhuman. Violence against the subhuman is not violence as such; it is not only tolerable but permissible. For Afropessimists, this means that "the violence that both elaborates and saturates Black 'life' is totalizing, so much so as to make [redemptive] narrative inaccessible to Blacks."[15]

The utter depravity antiblack violence exposes about the ideology of white supremacy, on full display in spectacle lynchings in the early part of the twentieth century, mirrors spectacle aspects of Black violent death on display in recorded police shootings of unarmed Black men and women in the early twenty-first century. What these events demonstrate is the extent to which violent antiblackness is systemic and a fundamental tenet of American whiteness. They demonstrate the inadequacy and ineffectiveness of the traditional Christian symbol, the cross, intended to offer

14. Wilderson, *Afropessimism*, 226.
15. Wilderson, *Afropessimism*, 226.

hope and empowerment and to represent restraint, moral conviction and universal love to Black and white Christians.

Beginning in the 1890s, spectacle lynchings are a symbol of the systemic, racist rot at the heart of whiteness. They were not the impetuous actions of a white mob performing criminal acts they hoped to conceal in order to subvert punishment and accountability; what makes them spectacle events is that they were carefully planned and "could not have happened without widespread knowledge and the explicit sanction of local and state authorities and with the tacit approval from the federal government, members of the white media, churches, and universities."[16] In most cases, spectacle lynchings were announced in advance by way of newspapers and other media. At these events, in addition to being hanged, the Black victim often would be burned for hours. White onlookers would revel in the desecration and defilement of a Black human being and take home parts of the body as souvenirs: genitals, fingers, toes, ears, and so forth. They would create postcards of the event and other mementos. Why was it necessary for them to memorialize, to reflect fondly on, a public execution-turned-picnic? Some Black scholars have noted that whites often lynched Blacks merely to "remind the Black community of their powerlessness."[17] Put another way, it was to remind them of their subhuman existence, their continued status as property.

The public spectacle of Black powerlessness in violent antiblackness continues on display after the civil rights and Black Power movements helped to end spectacle lynching. In 2021, white police shootings and choking deaths of unarmed Black citizens are the spectacle lynchings of the twenty-first century and symbolize the constancy of Black social death. They are

16. Cone, *Cross and the Lynching Tree,* 9.
17. Cone, *Cross and the Lynching Tree,* 12.

spectacles to the extent that they are public events, recorded on cell phone video for the entire nation to witness over and over through television and social media. And they are similarly systemic in that they are the continued result of coordinated efforts on the part of the American criminal justice system to shelter white nationalists disguised as police officers. These are not merely the actions of a few impassioned and fearful cops; they are coordinated efforts by a criminal justice system, including prosecutors, judges, juries, and lawmakers conspiring to render Black bodies non-beings, non-humans. Legal protections like qualified immunity and specious claims of fearing for one's life function to provide a canopy of justification around white supremacist violence.

In 2014, Tamir Rice was a twelve-year-old boy shot and killed within twenty seconds of police officers arriving at the scene, for playing with a toy gun in a public park in Cleveland, Ohio. A grand jury would later fail to indict the officer, because it appeared to them that Rice was wielding a weapon. The police officer would eventually be fired three years later, not for shooting Rice, but for not revealing to Cleveland police that at his previous job as a police officer in Independence, Ohio, he had been deemed an emotionally unstable recruit.

In the same year, in the New York City borough of Staten Island, Eric Garner was choked to death by police officers, a public spectacle lynching recorded on video, for selling individual cigarettes and expressing resentment for continually being harassed by the police for selling those cigarettes on the corner. His last words, which have become an indelible mantra for Black Lives Matter activists, were "I can't breathe." Similar to Rice's case, a grand jury refused to indict the officers in the Eric Garner case despite the medical examiner's ruling of Garner's death as a homicide. These are merely two examples among many others (e.g., John Crawford, Trayvon Martin, Breonna Taylor, George Floyd, Alston Sterling, Jacob Blake) of the current manifestation of vicious antiblack violence that continues unabated 156 years after the official end of American chattel slavery, and over fifty years after the Black Power movement and the emergence of Black liberation theology.

Like spectacle lynchings of a century ago, these twenty-first-century lynchings are no less a reminder of Black powerlessness in America, no less a reminder that Black people continue to exist as *no-citizens*, as *aftermath property*. These violent acts of antiblackness similarly terrorize as lynchings in reminding Black people, in the words of Christina Sharpe, that we have "no nation or state to protect us, with no citizenship bound to be respected." And like the casual(?) burning of defiled Black bodies at spectacle lynchings, the constant replaying of Black killings by law enforcement in the media—Black trauma pornography—desensitizes the viewing public and normalizes antiblack violence and death. Black liberation theology lacks the proper theological language, the proper vocabulary, religious symbols, or categories to address the rot at the core of whiteness and to empower Black people to discern their reality for what it is. Our continued reliance on the cross as the central Christian symbol and the universal representation of redemptive suffering has done nothing to transform Black powerlessness or quell white antiblack violence but actually works to pacify and mitigate Black anger and righteous indignation.

President Barack Obama's eulogy in the aftermath of the racist shooting deaths of the Emanuel Nine serves as an illustration of the Black church's theological impotence and the role redemptive suffering plays in Black pacification, too often providing shelter for white antiblack violence. On the night of Wednesday, June 25, 2015, in Charleston, South Carolina, a young white man visited the Emanuel African Methodist Episcopal Church to attend Bible study at this Black church. He was welcomed with open arms despite his racial otherness and unfamiliarity to anyone in attendance. The young man sat through the entire gathering, and at the end, while the Black church members had their heads bowed and eyes closed during the closing prayer, he pulled out his gun and shot and murdered nine of them, including the pastor of the church, Rev. Clementa Pinckney. The shooter was a self-proclaimed white nationalist. In the initial aftermath of the church shooting, it is noteworthy that Christian forgiveness was the idea immediately invoked by the family members of the victims in the assailant's first court hearing. Many family members offered the white gunman forgiveness despite his failure to exhibit contrition, accept responsibility, or offer repentance.

At the funeral for the victims, President Obama delivered the eulogy, in which he invoked the concept of redemptive suffering through his sermon about the theological concept of grace. The innocence of the victims, the Emanuel Nine, as with the death of Jesus, ensures God's participation in making this an event of redemption. According to Obama, the shooter had one intention, "But God works in mysterious ways. God has different ideas. He [the white domestic terrorist] didn't know that he was being used by God."[18] Like Niebuhr, Obama invokes a central Protestant theological claim that God can redeem evil and transform it into good, the evidence of which is the cross of Jesus. But in making the claim the way he does, is not Obama assigning agency and intentionality to God in the deaths of the nine innocent Black victims? What is also apparent in Obama's remarks is how this theology shifts the focus and priority away

---

18. President Barack Obama, "Amazing Grace," eulogy for Reverend Clementa Pinckney, delivered at the College of Charleston, June 26, 2015.

from the nine Black victims to the shooter as protagonist in God's drama, just a cog in the fulfillment of God's mysterious "plan." Obama's eulogy at this funeral during this Black Christian ritual of mourning-turned-spectacle, as it was broadcast to a national television audience, was itself a celebration of the capacity of Black people to suffer incessantly without redress or even demands for white contrition or repentance. If God was using the shooter to further God's plan, the eulogy seemed to imply, then is not the shooter an agent of God, perhaps advancing God's plan of racial reconciliation in America? If so, when and where is the resurrection-like historical evidence to prove that this particular instance of Black suffering was truly redemptive/good?

Offering analysis of the eulogy, Michael Eric Dyson notes that Obama's declaration "doesn't mean that God intended Roof to do wrong; it means that God uses even Roof's bad actions for good purposes, purposes that were lost to Roof behind his veil of evil."[19] But what are those good purposes? Where is the good result demonstrating that the shooter was being used by God in furtherance of some divine plan ultimately beneficial to Black people? Dyson goes on to discuss the removal of the Confederate flag from the state capitol in South Carolina. Is that the extent of the good purposes? Does that small, long-overdue, symbolic gesture justify the murder of nine Black human beings? *How* did God use this racist, white attacker? Rather, what President Obama actually did was trade on his celebrity and leverage a traditional Black Christian theological trope to pacify Black outrage, as head of the white supremacist state, and prevent potential violent racial clashes that could have resulted from this act of antiblack violence and white domestic terrorism.

19. Michael Eric Dyson, *The Black Presidency: Barack Obama and the Politics of Race in America* (Boston: Houghton Mifflin Harcourt, 2016), 268.

He used the theological vocabulary available to him in that context, exacerbating the empathy gulf between Black and white people by placing himself front and center at a festival of Black misery, revealing the contours and depth of Black social death.

Obama closes the sermon by singing the refrain of the hymn "Amazing Grace" to thunderous applause. He invokes a hymn, written by a man who participated in the warehousing and transportation of enslaved Africans on a slave ship, at a Black funeral necessitated by white supremacist violence. Grace for the undeserving sinner as demonstrative of the human condition convinces Black Christians to forgive as they would want forgiveness and allows the pathology of whiteness to be obfuscated and even ignored. Obama proclaimed, "If we can find that grace, anything is possible. If we can tap that grace, everything can change."[20] Black Christians perpetually demonstrate *amazing grace,* superhuman grace, for white people, even white terrorists, further perpetuating the awesome burden of Blacks as objects of suffering, unique superhuman sufferers. Wilderson argues that examples like this demonstrate why the "Black is a sentient being but not a Human being," because Black people have a different relationship to violence compared to other racial groups, even other oppressed groups. "The Human suffers contingent violence, violence that kicks in when he resists (or is perceived to resist) the disciplinary discourse of civil society's rules and laws. But Black people's saturation by violence is a paradigmatic necessity, not simply the performance of contingency."[21] The maintenance of whiteness requires violence against the Black body. It requires Black suffering. And Black Christians' appropriation of certain Christian symbols, like the cross, glorifies and places a sacred canopy on racial suffering,

---

20. Dyson, *Black Presidency*, 268.
21. Wilderson, *Afropessimism,* 245.

too often feeding and helping maintain whiteness through the projection of a God that honors, even requires, their Black suffering. "He didn't know that he was being used by [our] God." Obama projected a racist, religious caricature of Blackness and in so doing sidestepped the urgency of white repentance as well as his own leadership role in calling out and addressing systemic white supremacy. He became an accomplice in perpetuating the condition of Black social death.

What this exposes is that traditional Christian categories, like the cross, are not only woefully inadequate for subverting whiteness but actually help to maintain whiteness by appeasing Black rage and vitiating Black public discontent. This is not dissimilar to the basic critique of redemptive suffering that Malcolm X leveled against Martin Luther King's Jr.'s insistence that Black people love their oppressors. The famed psychologist Dr. Kenneth Clark agreed with Malcolm X that the requirement to love the oppressor placed an undue psychological burden on Black people that is deleterious to their mental health.[22] While Cone's Black theology distances itself from King's interpretation of the cross and his absolutism of nonviolence, Black theology has not rejected the symbol itself or made clear the connection between Black Christian embrace of it and continued acceptance of incursions of antiblack violence. Redemptive suffering through the cross of Jesus preempts the need for and importance of white repentance or reparation and increases the empathy gulf between many white and Black people. Too many white people cannot possibly imagine the power and the ability of Black people to endure such suffering, disrespect, and disregard. And their inability to imagine or empathize fully with Black suffering actually helps mitigate their white guilt and instantiate Black being as "other." Such dehumanization and "othering" are

22. Kenneth Clark, interview with Malcolm X, PBS, 1963.

both the essence of whiteness and the definition of Black social death. Wilderson concludes,

> Thus, like class and gender, which are also *constructs,* not divine designations, social death can be destroyed. But the first step toward the destruction is to assume one's position (assume, not celebrate or disavow), and then burn the ship or the plantation, in its past and present incarnations, from the inside out. However, as Black people we are often psychically unable and unwilling to assume this position.[23]

Black Christians' continued embrace of theological symbols that instantiate social death under the guise of a false universalism is the root problem.

THE ANCESTORS: ALTERNATIVE SYMBOLS

Burning the ship, or plantation, from the inside out means rejecting Christian symbols interpreted through the lens of whiteness (a manifestation of double-consciousness). Black people need different religious symbols and an expansive theological vocabulary. Sharpe suggests that those who engage the development of Black thought and/or work to ensure Black survival do so acknowledging the Black condition in the wake of the slave ship. She calls this *wake work.*[24] She admits she is in search of a language and a form to explain this work but recognizes that the contours must extend beyond the borders of the United States. She asserts, "We must be about the work of what I am calling wake work as a theory and praxis of the wake; a theory

---

23. Wilderson, *Afropessimism,* 103.
24. Sharpe, *In the Wake,* 19.

and a praxis of Black being in diaspora."[25] Wake work could
mean reimagining blackness by reconfiguring the spatial plane
for identity formation across the Atlantic Ocean, thus bridging the conceptual distance between American Blacks and pre-
Black existence and ancestral heritage in Africa (Africana). Part
of the condition of superhuman suffering is enhanced among
Black people because of minoritized status in America. This
minoritized status develops into a minoritized consciousness
often manifesting quietism and individualism and promoting
narratives of victimization. This is why one had to be a cow-
ard in the deep South during the period of lynching. It is a
consciousness, informed by experiences of utter powerlessness,
that eventually equates minoritized status with inferiority, with
the abnormal. But the reclamation of Black personhood and the
Earth demands the repudiation of minoritized consciousness
and opens the way back through the door of no-return, reminding Black people of their connection to a West African heritage.

I posit the ancestor as a category of meaning incorporated
within the *orthography of the wake*[26] that invites reconceptualization of Black life, loss, violence, death, and even salvation.
Because they reside in the natural world, the ancestors provide a
conceptual bridge linking racial suffering to the Earth's suffering and continental Africa with North America. In *Indigenous
Black Theology*, I argued that Black theology should incorporate
the West African notion of ancestor to reconcile with and overcome African American Christians' alienation from indigenous
African religions and culture. This is necessary in order to affirm
the truth that African people contributed to the development of
spiritual and theological knowledge that preceded their introduction to Western forms of Protestant Christianity as a con-

25. Sharpe, *In the Wake*, 19.
26. Sharpe, *In the Wake*, 20.

sequence of the transatlantic slave trade and slavery. Otherwise the theological claim that Jesus is the unique, exclusive savior for all threatens to legitimize Black people's racial inferiority and their reliance on white religious instruction in antebellum America.

Ancestor works as a more relevant and effective theological symbol than the cross, revealing the connection between the legacy of white antiblack violence committed against Black bodies and the Earth. Reclaiming Black space(s) means bridging the conceptual distance between Black Americans and Africa, overcoming the "negative distance" between African Americans and indigenous African culture, idioms, and modalities.[27] This *negative distance* was necessitated, in America's postbellum period, by Black people's embrace of a Protestant Christian theological explanation for slavery based on the doctrine of providence. Black Christian accommodationist theology viewed slavery as part of God's providential design for civilizing and Christianizing the Negro. This theology claims that Black people needed to be raised up from their "pagan" origins. It is another early example of how Black Christian theologizing caters to white fragility, guilt, and insecurity by ultimately vindicating whites of their barbarity in racialized chattel slavery. God allowed slavery in order to redeem African Americans and ultimately continental Africans. If this is true, then indigenous African religions with their various idioms, symbols, and modalities emerge as the great villain, the evil of fetishism from which Black people should be purged. My work rejects these claims and calls for a recovery and reconstruction of specific African idioms, categories, and symbols, such as ancestor, so they can become relevant to a twenty-first-century Africana reality.

27. Dianne M. Stewart, *Three Eyes for the Journey: African Dimensions of the Jamaican Religious Experience* (New York: Oxford University Press, 2005).

The ancestors are a living reality and a metaphor for the unity of all existence that connects the spiritual, invisible plane with the natural, visible one. They also remind us to value the spiritual principle of *reciprocity*.

> In sum, all the plural spiritual realities that constitute African cosmological systems, whether the Supreme God, the less divinities, or the ancestors, all exist, function, and operate within the same temporal/spatial realm as the living, visible human beings. Because of this, there is a single unity, a mutuality and sense of reciprocal obligation that exists between the natural and the spiritual, and the visible and the invisible worlds. One is not under the subjection of the other, but they both, in fact, need one another for their proper functioning and harmonious existence. Reciprocal obligation has the highest value because the entire system depends on the basis of this relationality. The visible world gives voice, substance, and tangibility to the invisible world, and the visible world depends upon the invisible for health, protection, and sustenance. The ancestors are central to this relationality, because they, in fact, establish the basis for it.[28]

The ancestors help link Black suffering to the Earth's suffering. It is also a concept constitutive of the sacred value of memory requiring us to face and honor our tempestuous racial past. Ancestors are living beings precisely because they are remembered. Their names are invoked and their presence summoned long after their visible presence is no more. Conversely, "Hell is

---

28. Jawanza Eric Clark, *Indigenous Black Theology: Toward an African-Centered Theology of the African-American Religious Experience* (New York: Palgrave Macmillan, 2012), 78.

the state of not being remembered." It is when one becomes a lonely wandering spirit existing in total isolation and alienation from any community.

For Black people in America, the murders of Clementa Pinckney, Tamir Rice, Breonna Taylor, and Eric Garner, among others, call out for accountability and must be honored through our memory and constant invocation of their names. Their deaths were spectacle lynchings and the result of vicious white antiblack violence. We might posit them as hero ancestors, not because they were famed public figures of great excellence in life, but because they embodied Blackness in its quotidian forms in life, yet in death symbolize the ongoing terrorism marking Black social death in America and calling out for reciprocal obligation through ritual repentance. Calling their names invokes their energy and presence and forces us to wrestle with the necessity to honor them through a racial reckoning. They exemplify the precarious nature of Black existence in America and demand that we restore harmony and balance to the spaces their spirits continue to occupy. Unlike the theodicy of redemptive suffering, God does not overshadow or even erase white culpability by turning something intended for evil into something good. God cannot clean this stench through a theology that misremembers and distorts the actors of these dramas by purifying evildoers and transforming them into agents of God. The pouring of libations as a ritual of healing, remembrance, and invocation of the ancestors invites us to return to the scene of the crime, return to the spaces disrespected and disregarded through our own willful forgetfulness, and restore balance and harmony to the space. The ritual of pouring water or stronger beverages on the ground both consecrates that little portion of Earth and summons the presence of ancestor(s) to the ritual space.

In the case of the Emanuel Nine, this healing ritual would require returning to the church ground. In the case of Tamir

Rice, it calls for returning to the public park in Cleveland, Ohio. For Trayvon Martin and Eric Garner, we would return to the sidewalks in Sanford, Florida, and Staten Island, New York, respectively and invoke their energies through ritual libations. We remember them. We say their names! We honor the spaces they inhabit. These acts of remembrance and invocation fortify those who live in the aftermath, begin a process of healing, and increase resolve to confront antiblackness and white violence. It does not vitiate the anger or quell the rage, but it helps us to see ourselves and white antiblackness clearly.

Ancestor, as a theological category, enables us to see death anew. Death is not punishment for sin, as St. Augustine insisted, nor does it signify the end of our existence in this spatiotemporal field. But death is a stage of transition that "comes and is accepted as necessary to the truth of life, and as a source of solidarity, communication, and reciprocity among the living."[29] Not only do ancestors exist within a state of reciprocal obligation to the living, but their spirit, or energies, return in their descendants. We are literally our ancestors. And, as such, we carry within us the intelligence, perseverance, fortitude, trauma, and proclivities of those who preceded us. We carry the high blood pressure and the predisposition for other health maladies in our genetic makeup. The enslaved Africans who died during the Middle Passage live inside of us. Slavery's *unresolved unfolding* manifests itself not only in double-consciousness and second-sight but also in the trauma stored in Black bodies. Black people carry in them the energies of their ancestors, and those energies cry out for acknowledgment and redress. Energy is neither created nor destroyed; thus, death does not signal an end but merely a state of transformation. And the natural world is the receptacle that stores this unacknowledged ancestral energy

---

29. Clark, *Indigenous Black Theology,* 91.

in Black bodies, but also in trees, rivers, hills, lakes … even sidewalks.

Ancestor as a theological category is an effective symbol for incorporation within a spatially oriented theology. Ancestors belie a Western temporal fixation, because they collapse time into the eternal now. The ancestors lived as visible humans in the past yet are present, contemporaneous realities in us and all around us. Through them, the past both simultaneously empowers and haunts and stalks us. The present has enveloped the past and cannot be buried in the intentional forgetfulness of temporal, linear consciousness. Invoking the presence of ancestors means honoring, restoring, reclaiming, and reestablishing balance in the space(s) we all occupy. This spatial theology, then, is not reducible to the single narrative enshrined in the Bible about a Palestinian Jew who lived two thousand years ago. Ancestors as a theological symbol encourage an Africanizing, or indigenizing, of space(s) leading to confrontation with an ugly racial past and ecological recovery.

The Bible as Religious Symbol?

In *Indigenous Black Theology*, I decouple the doctrine of Jesus Christ from the doctrine of salvation, arguing that the concept of ancestors creates an ethical standard of the exemplary life as a better criterion for determining what salvation means. As a result, a multiplicity of beings, as opposed to one, achieve and model salvation. I construct a doctrine of Jesus Christ that understands him as a hero ancestor—not unlike Nat Turner, Denmark Vesey, or Martin Luther King Jr. and Malcolm X— and as a man who was lynched and killed, fighting to deliver an oppressed nation from their oppressors through an ethics of resistance. When viewed through an African-centered lens of struggle, it is clear that the messianic expectation is the anticipation of the Jewish ancestor, King David, returning in the form of a deliverer, the messiah. Jesus would later embrace the title, although he resisted the provincial and elitist way in which most Jews imagined it. He shattered the model, subverting their expectations, and forced a new definition of messianism upon them. I agree with Delores Williams that Jesus's salvific power lies in what he accomplished in his life, not his death. His death was a public execution, a lynching. His murder was *the sin of defilement*.[30] Williams's interpretation within an African-centered framing means that Jesus became a hero ancestor, one who lived an exemplary life of service, sacrifice, healing, and care for others.

Reinterpreting Jesus's life, mission, and death in light of an African-centered reading of the Gospels demands that we reconsider the Bible and how it will function as a source for this theology. Can, or rather should, the Bible be a key theological symbol for a spatially oriented, Africana ecotheology? Historically, Black Christians have approached the Bible in a way that reveals a component feature of whiteness. They too often approached the text as an objective edifice of truth merely in need of a proper interpretation. As a result, the Bible became an idol, a fetish even, instead of a sacred text written by flawed human beings reflecting their own cultural biases. The idea that the Bible is the "Word of God" is a manifestation of white epistemological hubris and an inherent endorsement of domination ideologies like the notion of the elect or chosen people. We might rather embrace the idea that we must interpret the Bible, if we are to interpret it at all, from our own culturally biased perspective and dispense with the notion that it can be read objectively or that it posits one central theme or claim. There

---

30. Delores S. Williams, *Sisters in the Wilderness: The Challenge of Womanist God-Talk* (Maryknoll, NY: Orbis Books, 1993).

is not one God but several gods, or God-symbols, revealed in the Bible. There is not one theodicy but several theodicies, not one theology but multiple theologies. How do we read the Bible such that it serves as a pragmatic tool to help fight oppression; and, if it cannot serve in this way, should we not rid ourselves of it once and for all?

Sylvester Johnson argues that the Bible is an ethically ambivalent text embracing ideologies of domination and that it should never have been used as the basis upon which to decide significant societal issues such as the morality of slavery. He makes this claim by offering a historical account of how nineteenth-century Americans fashioned arguments based on their interpretation of scripture both to justify American chattel slavery and to repudiate it. The Bible was used both by abolitionists and by pro-slavery advocates, each relying on their own selected scriptures to either defend or reject the institution of slavery. In both instances, their ability to persuade their readers or listeners required appropriating biblical scripture. According to Johnson, "Because so few individuals ever conceived of challenging the Bible itself, religious debates over slavery typically concerned what the Bible meant and not the problem of human brutality, per se."[31]

This preoccupation with proper interpretation of scripture, instead of human brutality itself, is particularly problematic when one considers the narrative of the curse of Ham in the book of Genesis and all the ways that both abolitionists and pro-slavery advocates have assumed the legitimacy of the narrative. Johnson notes that the Puritan judge Samuel Sewall and abolitionist Samuel Hopkins each attempt to explain why

31. Sylvester A. Johnson, "The Bible, Slavery, and the Problem of Authority," in *Beyond Slavery: Overcoming Its Religious and Sexual Legacies*, ed. Bernadette J. Brooten (New York: Palgrave Macmillan, 2010), 231.

the curse should not apply to Black people in bondage in the nineteenth century. Sewall argued that no one knows if Noah's curse is still in effect and that Noah cursed Ham's descendants, not Ham himself. Hopkins claimed that Black people were not, in fact, descendants of Ham but descendants of other sons of Noah. Hopkins also posited that God gave the Israelites, God's chosen people, special instructions and permissions that did not apply to other people (non-Jews/gentiles), so acts of brutality and immorality for which the Israelites were not held accountable were also not applicable to white Christians in America. Johnson references Hopkins to make the point that none of the late-eighteenth- and early-nineteenth-century biblical interpreters questioned the Bible itself or this narrative specifically. Why is there a narrative in the sacred text about Ham's descendants being cursed because of what amounted to a simple mistake on the part of Ham? Why would the penalty be so severe for what amounts to a mild indiscretion? Was it not Noah's fault in the first place for being drunk and naked and susceptible to discovery by his youngest son? Why include this narrative in the Bible at all? Could it be the story provides justification for the Israelite genocide of the Canaanites, since the Canaanites were Ham's immediate descendants, according to the text? Perhaps this story is in the Bible to provide cover and a weak rationale for the Israelites' horrific treatment of another people in the name of God. It therefore establishes an ideology of domination, a statement about who matters in the text and who does not, who this God does or does not care about.

> The Bible is a cultural tool, a vehicle for imposing a particular meaning on the world. It is the product of human activity that is chiefly concerned with maintaining a particular vision of the world. We must never allow biblical debates to mislead us into thinking that

the Bible is the issue and that all will be well if we can only extract its pristine truth. The Bible is not the issue. Social power is the issue. For this reason, interpreters of scripture bear an ethical responsibility to show readers that scripture is not an innocent category—it is always concerned with asserting a vision of social order whether or not that vision of order serves the interests of social victims.[32]

The suggestion that the Bible often asserts a vision in opposition to what is useful to *social victims* is a particular concern for Black theology and all theologies of liberation that rely on the Bible as a primary source.

Itumeleng Mosala proposes a subversive reading of scripture, because the claim that the Bible demonstrates that God is always on the side of the oppressed is contradicted by narratives like the curse of Ham, among many others. Mostly criticizing South African Black theologians, Mosala argues that Black theologians' appropriation of the Bible as the "Word of God" makes them ideological slaves to white epistemological hubris, and what Mosala calls an idealist epistemology. It is a way of understanding scripture that assumes the text is an objectively true, pure source for doing theology. Mosala makes his point this way:

I attempt to show that the fundamental problem underlying the present impotence of Black theology lies in its hermeneutical captivity to the ideological assumptions of white theology and Western civilization. These assumptions are reflected in the idealist epistemology characteristic of white theology and Western culture. The notion that the Bible is simply the revealed "Word

32. Johnson, "Bible, Slavery, and the Problem of Authority," 245.

of God" is an example of an exegetical framework that is rooted in such an idealist epistemology. I criticize that position in this study because it leads to the false notion of the Bible as nonideological, which can cause political paralysis in the oppressed people who read it.[33]

Mosala posits a historical materialist reading of the Bible based on the idea that "the struggle" is the key category for framing a Black hermeneutics of liberation. A renewed focus on space applied to biblical interpretation reveals within scripture contestations over land that has been appropriated by colonizers and imperialists to provide sacred justification for their hegemonic actions. In South Africa, the Dutch and the British used the Bible, particularly the exodus story and the book of Joshua, as a defense for conquest. Arguing that the whites in South Africa misinterpret the text misses the point and continues the problem of assigning innocence to the text itself. It would be better to make clear, as Mosala does, that "not all the Bible is on the side of human rights or of oppressed and exploited peoples."[34] The exodus narrative, which has often been a key scriptural component of Black theology's assertion that God is on the side of the oppressed, ultimately conveys an ideology of domination that works as well, if not better, for white imperialists as it does for oppressed Blacks seeking liberation. The divinely sanctioned genocide of the Canaanites cannot be justified as the problem of the reader or excused through exclusive identification with the Israelites as protagonists of scripture. Because of this, "oppressive texts cannot be totally tamed and subverted into liberating texts."[35]

---

33. Itumeleng J. Mosala, *Biblical Hermeneutics and Black Theology in South Africa* (Grand Rapids, MI: Eerdmans, 1989), 6.
34. Mosala, *Biblical Hermeneutics and Black Theology*, 30.
35. Mosala, *Biblical Hermeneutics and Black Theology*, 30.

Robert Warrior, representing a Native American perspective, long ago argued that the exodus narrative is an inappropriate and dangerous way for oppressed people to think about liberation. Based on the history of white imperialism in North America, Native Americans' lived experience is most reflective of the Canaanites, the conquered and vanquished victims of the exodus narrative. Warrior notes that most liberation theologians tend to ignore Yahweh's command to annihilate them, the indigenous people of the land. He also makes the point that the Canaanites who do survive "trusted in the God of outsiders and their story of oppression and exploitation was lost."[36] He rightly raises the question of what oppressed people are made to give up when they identify with the conquerors, "the winners," in order to gain some honorary status within the dominant society. Assimilation means rejecting one's own indigenous cultural narratives and resources and embracing someone else's story.

Perhaps a Black hermeneutics of struggle should be informed by the necessity of the oppressed community to own their own cultural biases in the reading of the text. Instead of trying to subvert them in the name of a false objectivity or false purity, cultural biases could be affirmed in order to transform the Bible into a weapon or mechanism in furtherance of Black liberation and survival. Randall Bailey warns of the dangers of failing to consider one's own cultural biases in interpreting scripture, such as when it results in oppressed people interpreting scripture from the perspective of the oppressor. In the case of African-descended people, this means reading the text through a Eurocentric lens. According to Bailey,

---

36. Robert Allen Warrior, "Canaanites, Cowboys, and Indians: Deliverance, Conquest, and Liberation Theology Today," *Christianity and Crisis* (September 11, 1989), 265.

> Along with adopting the language world of the text, we
> have also adopted the Eurocentric reading and interpre-
> tation of the text in many instances, so much so that we
> have lost our own story in the process. In other words,
> we have been trained to read the stories in ways that
> support the way whites read them and interpret them,
> which can run counter to our own psychic, spiritual,
> physical, and emotional well-being.[37]

Bailey notes, for example, that, as a people who were stolen from Africa and who have had land stolen from us here in
America as a consequence of white mob violence and terrorism,
Black Americans often fail to be critical of the biblical story
that is based on the promise to give Abraham's descendants land
belonging to someone else. We tend to identify with Abraham,
the protagonist of the story and the character with whom the
biblical writers most identify. Like Native Americans, African
Americans have more in common with the Canaanites than
with the Israelites in this particular narrative.

If we apply a spatial reading to the text, we see how much
of the Bible—the Pauline works in the New Testament notwithstanding—describes contestations about space, struggles
over land. The Jewish covenant grants the children of Abraham,
Isaac, and Jacob a piece of land they struggled to maintain, possess, and strive upon from the moment of conquest, through the
Babylonian captivity, and even during colonization by Rome.
Whether they attained and maintained God's favor was directly
correlated with the degree of their independent control and
ownership of the land, their stolen space. This is actually the

---

37. Randall Bailey, "The Danger of Ignoring One's Own Cultural Bias
in Interpreting the Test," in *The Postcolonial Bible*, ed. R. S. Sugirtharajah,
Bible and Postcolonialism 1 (Sheffield: Sheffield Academic Press, 1998), 78.

basis for the Jewish doctrine of election. Election, the Jews as God's chosen people, establishes the inherent partiality of the God(s) of scripture. Consequently, there is not a universal love of all people in scripture. There are winners and losers, oppressed and marginalized groups, and the biblical writers are not always writing with the needs of the victims in mind.

Renita Weems makes the point better:

> The premise here is simple: until criticism takes seriously the biblical peoples pervasive belief in their election and their understanding of what it means to be elected (the people of God), then we have not begun to resist the ideological foundation of the patriarchal world order, its ordering of society and its view of a select few in society in relation to the cosmos and the rest of the world.[38]

Election contravenes the African and Native American view of the Earth as an ecosystem in which each element must maintain balance and harmony. And the ease with which Black Christians identify with "the select few" in scripture, with the protagonists, means that the book can be used by oppressors in much the same way. What is worse is that this failure to deconstruct *election* renders the book a more likely weapon in the maintenance of our own oppression. Yet this traditional reading of the book continues to be a vital and primary source for Black and Womanist theology.

Bailey goes on to note how most Black Christians insist on promoting the Bible's innocence regarding positions on sexuality as well. He is critical of the willingness of most Black

---

38. Renita Weems, "Womanist Reflections on Biblical Hermeneutics," in *Black Theology: A Documentary History*, vol. 2, *1980–1992*, ed. James H. Cone and Gayraud S. Wilmore (Maryknoll, NY: Orbis Books, 1993), 221.

Christian churches to accept the sexual vilification of queer-identifying individuals, which occurs in certain Pauline texts (1 Timothy 1:10 and Romans 1:26–32), for example, despite Black American's history of being declared inferior based on a racist sexualization and the pervasive perpetuation of racist tropes of Black hypersexuality. Whether it is the Canaanites in the Hebrew Scriptures, or the gentiles and in some cases other Jews in the New Testament, Black Christians too easily accept injunctions against identifying with their "licentiousness and greed to practice every type of impurity" like fornication, and "we do not recognize our own story. We do not identify with the one or ones being maligned. Rather we identify with the mud-slinger."[39]

A subversive reading requires reading the text based on our cultural biases, even if that means questioning the elitist status and perspective of certain biblical writers. This requires us to make explicit decisions and choices about which texts to value and which to reject as counterproductive to our struggle. It means making some of the same political choices about texts that Howard Thurman's grandmother, a formerly enslaved person, made when she asked Howard to read scripture to her. Bailey calls this *a freedom of interpretation*[40] by which Thurman's grandmother would tell him not to read from certain Pauline texts, specifically those mandating that slaves be obedient to their masters. In so doing, she was rejecting that text, and others, as not canonical, sacred, or legitimate for her. She embraced her cultural bias, her sociohistorical perspective, regardless of the biblical writer's perspective, intent, or agenda. Paul's (or Pseudo-Paul's) perspective did not carry

---

39. Bailey, "Danger of Ignoring One's Own Cultural Bias," 79.
40. Bailey, "Danger of Ignoring One's Own Cultural Bias," 73.

more legitimacy than her own if his words contradicted or dismissed her lived experience.

Bailey's "freedom of interpretation" suggests that Black theology reinterrogate Albert Cleage's early interpretation of the Synoptic Gospels and their tension with the writings of the apostle Paul. Cleage argued that the gospel of Jesus was rooted in a gospel of liberation while Paul's theology was an individualistic gospel of salvation. While Cleage overstated his critique in ways that represent Jesus and Paul as too oppositional, or binary, he rightly draws attention to a tension in the New Testament between Jesus's theology of works and action, as represented in the Sermon on the Mount and the Beatitudes, and Paul's more abstract theology of faith. Based on the value of a "freedom of interpretation," the question for an oppressed people struggling to be free is, Is it more useful to the struggle to be told "Ask and it will be given to you; seek and you shall find; knock and the door will be open. For everyone who asks receives; the one who seeks finds; and the one who knocks, the door will be opened" (Matthew 7:7–8)? Or is it better to be told "So in Christ Jesus you are all children of God through faith, for all of you who were baptized into Christ have clothed yourselves with Christ. There is neither Jew nor gentile, neither slave nor free, nor is there male or female, for you are all one in Christ Jesus" (Galatians 3:26–28)? Cleage's critique of Paul was informed by his unabashed embrace of Black people's cultural context of American racial revolution in the late 1960s. He was not trying to offer a universally applicable, and presumably objective, approach to scripture but a Black Christian Nationalist approach asserting with clarity that there are portions of scripture that are useful for the liberation struggle of Black people and other sections that are clearly detrimental. He was not in the practice of trying to redeem the harmful texts based solely on the fact that someone decided to include them in what we call scripture. Despite this, Cleage was marginalized among academic Black theologians in part because he resisted the allure of whiteness, which demands that theological claims have universal appeal instead of pragmatic efficacy.

Ultimately I want to question the presumed indispensability of the Bible as a source for Black and other theologies of liberation. The assumption that it can function as the "Word of God," or as some objective source that just needs to be interpreted correctly, makes oppressed people beholden to the same narratives and symbols so easily used by oppressors to promote domination ideologies. Black Christians should extract narratives, idioms, and symbols rooted in their own cultural biases for pragmatic efficacy toward resistance to oppression and also relegate the text to a secondary status that ceases to trump the present, lived experiences and interactions within the current space(s) and the land/Earth on which we currently reside.

* * *

In summary, the task of this chapter was to demonstrate the inadequacy of specific traditional Christian symbols and their inability to meet the urgent need of addressing the persistence of antiblack violence, Black social death, and the constancy of whiteness. The cross, specifically the atonement achieved through Christ's death, is exposed as an insufficient symbol to encourage struggle against whiteness but rather instantiates Black suffering, actually deepening the divide between Black and white people in America. It does this by highlighting the penchant and tremendous capacity of Black people to suffer, in effect glorifying the Black body as superhuman sufferer. In so doing, Black Christian acceptance of the cross confirms Black social death instead of destroying it. As in the case of the Emanuel Nine, rather than indicting whiteness, the Black Christian embrace of the cross and redemptive suffering exonerates whiteness, specifically the violence at the core of whiteness, through obfuscation by a false universalism that essentially changes the subject or focus away from white violence, reducing it to a supporting role in God's unfolding drama, God's providential design. God's power to bring goodness out of evil if the victims suffer correctly obscures the necessity to hold white evildoers accountable.

Similarly, the Bible as a religious symbol helps manifest Black peoples' double-consciousness, specifically Blacks' embrace of whiteness through the appropriation of the Bible as the "Word of God," or the objective source of truth, and the ease with which Black interpreters identify with the so-called heroes of scripture, failing to view the narratives through their own cultural biases. Black theology must insist on a "freedom of interpretation" for the Bible to continue to function as a source for doing theology. Insistence on an objectively true or correct interpretation of the Bible exonerates the biblical writers, making Black Christians slaves to the domination ideologies within the text, and continues the tradition of trying to correct white interpretations such that oppressive texts read as liberative. But as Mosala demonstrates, "Oppressive texts cannot be totally tamed and subverted into liberating texts."

Finally, I propose the ancestors as a category that transcends the limits of blackness since they predate its construction. As a central religious symbol, they offer a new interpretation of the life and death of Jesus the Christ, point in the direction of an African-centered reading of the Bible, provide a more suitable symbol for a spatially focused theology, and speak to the urgent necessity to remember, honor, and redefine Black life and death in America. The ancestors demand that we honor the ground, the spaces, on which they made their transition from life to death back to life; through their memorial and invocation we not only begin the healing process but begin crafting a racial/ethnic identity circumventing the parameters of whiteness and the limitations of double-consciousness.

5

What Is Liberation?
A Reappraisal

The shift from a temporal, linear focus in theology to one that prioritizes the spatial requires a reexamination of the telos, or goal, of Black liberation theology specifically. We have already established that the Western preoccupation with the temporal places primacy on the idea of progress and linear movement. The notion of progress fuels the global, Western technological order, an order characterized by the mechanization and exploitation of nature, the land, the Earth. The act of progressing manifests hierarchical relations as one begins to characterize people, cultures, or worldviews as either progressive or regressive, evolved or primitive. In this sense, specific groups perceive themselves as superior to others as opposed to merely different from them.

Marimba Ani indicates that the European/Western notion of progress coincides "with the growth of the technical order while justifying political and cultural imperialism."[1] She notes that expansionism is implicit in the very idea of progress. Progress requires expansion and perpetual creation and consumption of products, possessions, land, and other objects. The past is consumed and discarded in an incessant march to an unattain-

---

1. Marimba Ani, *Yurugu: An African-centered Critique of European Cultural Thought and Behavior* (Trenton, NJ: Africa World Press, 1994), 490.

able future fueled by an insatiable desire for power and control over others. Neoliberalism is the offspring, a byproduct, of this Western view of progress with its belief in perpetual growth, glorification of individualism, and unlimited consumption of limited natural resources. Competition over those limited natural resources produces a winner-take-all, survivor-of-the-fittest mentality that blames "losers" for their own apparent inadequacies and failure to compete. Black people and Native Americans are characterized as the great losers of history, as anthropologically defective, not merely in socioeconomic terms but also as regards their cultural commitment to constantly acknowledge their connection to and dependency on land and the Earth, or land/Earth.

Black liberation theology has been critical of this ideology, often framing neoliberalism as a manifestation of whiteness. Black theology, like other forms of liberation theology, has sought to construct a system of thought deconstructing this Western preoccupation with progress and, in particular, the way progress is weaponized to argue that racial advancements have been slow yet steady since the enslavement of African peoples in the Western hemisphere. The myth of racial progress thwarts revolutionary action by encouraging reformist approaches to defeating racism and lends credence to the claims of Afropessimism that the perception of Black people in American society continues to be that of mere objects, the "afterlives of property." Yet Black theology aims to liberate people from white racial oppression. Blackness is defined as *oppressed existence struggling to be free.*[2] But a question remains: What does this freedom look like, and are not the telos of Black theology and the way that telos is conceptualized themselves infected with

2. James H. Cone, *A Black Theology of Liberation* (Maryknoll, NY: Orbis Books, 1970).

some of the assumptions imbedded in Western liberalism? Is
Black theology's goal of liberation itself conceptualized within
a temporal orientation tied to the notion of Western progress?
Ani claims, "It is common for one committed to 'the Western
way' to express concern over where 'it' is all leading, and yet to
be convinced of his obligation to 'take it' there; to bestow the
leadership of his culture upon those 'less fortunates' who do not
know the way."[3] What is liberation in Black theology? Where is
it all leading? And what happens after we arrive, if we arrive at
all? How will we know when we have arrived, when it has been
achieved? What does liberation look like?

Contestation over the goal of liberation and the meaning
behind the concept itself has been at the root of much dispute
and theological tension among various forms of liberation theology. It formed the basis for early disagreements between North
American Black theology and African theology, particularly as
represented in the criticisms of John S. Mbiti. At the core of this
dispute was a disagreement about the goal and thus the methodology of Black liberation theology. It also formed part of the
basis of Womanist theologians' critique of the "black androcentrism" within Black theology.

I argue that the problem of progress, as informed by a theological preoccupation with the temporal, led Black theology to
incorporate a Westernized understanding of liberation framed
also by a biblical view of reality. The shift to a theological prioritization of the spatial demands a reconceptualization of the
meaning of "liberation," placing renewed stress on restoring
balance and harmony to the spatial plane as much as political liberation. Additionally, this shift demands that land/Earth
be included as a central theological symbol requiring that we
rethink, or redefine, "liberation." Womanist and African eco-

3. Ani, *Yurugu*, 491.

feminist theologies advance this reconceptualization as well. Liberation has to involve more than just the political economy. It must necessitate restoration of the Earth, specifically the land, which has been despiritualized and objectified. Our present space(s) must be restored and renewed in the here and now, not in some future eschatological or liberation event.

First-generation Black theologians tended to define liberation in ways related almost exclusively to the political economy, presuming that the concept had to do fundamentally with improving the socioeconomic conditions of Black people. Yet there was always a question among some Black theologians of whether capitalism was the proper vehicle for achieving *liberation.* In *For My People,* James Cone is highly critical of the civil rights movement's goal of integration, arguing that it consists simply of Blacks seeking inclusion within a capitalistic society in decline. According to him, "We [Black people] need political intelligence that is sophisticated enough to move beyond the dream of integration into a decaying capitalist economy. No human being should want to integrate into a structure that systematically destroys the poor and enriches the rich."[4] Cone was influenced by Cornel West and, even before West, by his travels to African, Asian, and Latin American countries, where his engagement with Third World theologians helped him develop his Marxist analysis.

Cornel West, of course, famously critiqued Black theology for its absence of systemic social analysis, or social theory, "which impedes [Black theologians] from putting forward a precise idea of what constitutes socioeconomic and political liberation."[5]

4. James H. Cone, *For My People: Black Theology and the Black Church* (Maryknoll, NY: Orbis Books, 1984), 200.
5. Cornel West, "Black Theology of Liberation as Critique of Capitalist Civilization," in *Black Theology: A Documentary History*, vol. 2, *1980–1992*,

Were some Black theologians positing Black capitalism as a form of liberation? West is the one who proposed that Black theologians and progressive Marxists become conversation partners. He also called for a clearer explication of Black economic powerlessness, which is directly related to racism and the legacy of white supremacy but is not entirely reducible to it, because Black economic powerlessness also stems from a lack of control of the means of production. In this sense, the vast majority of white people are also powerless and economically exploited. The question for him is, How do Black people have a say in the decision-making processes of the institutions that control their lives upon which they are dependent? West thought that Black theology's exclusive focus on race, racial injustice, and the legacy of white supremacy obscured a pressing need for a class analysis that also worked to distance Black people in America and their *Black experience* from Black and brown people in the so-called Third World. Absent from Black theology was a critique of Western globalization and imperialistic land conquest, and an analysis of how power operated. He accused Black theologians of too often confusing power with high wages. To that end, West called for democratically controlled institutions where the people, the folk, "participate in their decision-making processes."[6] He argued further that, if Black theologians were unwilling to discuss this, the term *liberation* was "meretricious" and should be replaced with *inclusion*, because what liberation really equates to is American, middle-class status and consciousness.[7]

West's critique led to deeper engagement with progressive Marxism and with Marxist analysis in Black theology. I argue

---

ed. James H. Cone and Gayraud S. Wilmore (Maryknoll, NY: Orbis Books, 1993), 415.

6. Cornel West, *Prophesy Deliverance! An Afro-American Revolutionary Christianity* (Philadelphia: Westminster, 1982), 114.

7. West, *Prophesy Deliverance!*, 112.

that consideration of the land, the legacy of racist land dispossession, and the need for land recovery and restoration could serve as a possible missing link, or a bridge, connecting racial to class analysis in Black theology. If the land/Earth were to be elevated to a crucial and primary theological symbol it could be used to connect Black theology's racial analysis to the legacy of Western/European imperialism, as well as to concern for ecological exploitation and destruction.

Cone would later affirm the necessity of Marxism and Marxist analysis for the Black community and the Black church. In particular, he recommended Marx's critique of religion, especially religion's tendency to immerse itself in abstract thought, its dehistoricizing tendencies, and the lack of pragmatic impact on the lives of everyday people. It is this aspect of Marxist thought that many Latin American liberation theologians found poignant and relevant for their context. Of course, Marxism never got fair consideration in the Black church owing to Marxism's embrace of atheism, its demonization within American society generally, and the fear on the part of Black church leadership of the white reaction to Black Christians' embrace of Marxism. Problematically, the Black Panther Party stands out as an example of a Black organization that embraced Marxism and was vilified in the government and white media outlets, leading to their marginalization in the Black community, constant governmental surveillance through COINTELPRO (Counter Intelligence Program), and eventual dismantling.

Yet Black theologians called for a reconceptualization of Marxism, not simply in terms of the doctrines of the church but, most importantly, because of its critique of political economy and the system of capitalism.

> The new social order should be democratic and social-
> ist, including a Marxist critique of monopoly capital-

ism. It must also be a socialism that is critical of the
authoritarian state socialism (Soviet Russia). Just as we
should not reject Christianity because churches carry
its name but do the opposite of what the faith stands
for, likewise we should not reject socialism just because
[other nations] adopted the name but did the opposite.
The new social order must view the necessities of life—
food, shelter, work, play—as rights inalienably linked
with membership in society. No one, absolutely no one,
should control the wealth of a nation or community
through the private ownership of property.[8]

Here Cone calls for a reimagining of Marxism that is predicated primarily on his critique of religion and capitalism. Of
course, I question whether Marx and Marxism ultimately
fetishize the political economy, even as Marx rightly critiques
the social constructions of "commodities" and "capital." Marx
is right to point out the extent to which capitalism becomes a
religion through its idolization of capital, glorification of profit
motive, and emphasis on conspicuous material accumulation.
Yet Marxism clearly has its limitations, and something is missing from this vision of liberation. Marx's analysis suffers from
being framed exclusively within a Eurocentric context and
paradigm that too often ignored the need for enslaved Africans
and the vicious land dispossession that were instrumental to
the development of capitalism. Marxism, after all, is a Western
construct. As Cedric Robinson notes, "It is a conceptualization
of human affairs and historical development that is emergent
from the historical experiences of European peoples mediated,
in turn, through their civilization, their social orders, and their

---

8. Cone, *For My People*, 204.

cultures."[9] He goes on to remark, "Racialism ... ran deep in the bowels of Western culture, negating its varying social relations of production and distorting their inherent contradictions."[10] Marx's racial blind spot is explained more succinctly by J. Lorand Matory:

> Marx's binary classification of the actors under capitalism—capitalists and proletariat—appears to reflect his personal social experience, his hopes, and his fears. He minimized and even actively denied the contemporaneous existence, labor, subjectivity, and importance of a third class: the tens of millions of mainly African or African-descended enslaved people whose labor was integral to the process through which Europeans and Euro-American capitalists, according to Marx himself, falsely imagined that their money was, by itself, giving birth to more money. Marx also imagined out of existence a range of other actors in this system, including the Native Americans whose land was appropriated for the founding of Marx's much-idealized United States of America, which he described as "virgin soil colonized by free immigrants."[11]

Marxist analysis, while useful in calling to account the inherent inequity and individualistic greed that feeds and enables capitalism, refuses to account for the Earth and the violations performed to the land by European and Euro-American capitalists. It is the fetishism of capital that undergirds reductive, even

9. Cedric J. Robinson, *Black Marxism: The Making of the Black Radical Tradition* (Chapel Hill: University of North Carolina Press, 1983), 2.

10. Robinson, *Black Marxism*, 66.

11. J. Lorand Matory, *The Fetish Revisited: Marx, Freud, and the Gods Black People Make* (Durham, NC: Duke University Press, 2018), 46.

silly, conversations about United States reparations for slavery to African Americans, which too often devolve into disputes over the appropriate dollar amount and possible individual cash payouts. There is little to no appetite for more difficult discussion of the history of land loss, the legacy of spatial dislocation and confinement, or how the wages of whiteness lead to ecological disaster. In short, Marxism's utility in calling capitalism to account and proposing an alternative system—Marxist, socialist, or even some version of Black Power—intended to engender more fairness and economic equality, is also not necessarily liberation. And does Black theology dissolve once it has revolutionized the political economy?

This was the question epitomizing the conflict between first-generation North American Black theologians and African theologians when they met in the mid-1970s to collaborate regarding what was initially perceived to be a common experience and vision for theology. John S. Mbiti, a renowned Kenyan theologian, complained vociferously that a color-conscious theology is idolatrous, and he was also critical of the goal and theme of liberation in any theology. He warned, "What I view as an excessive preoccupation with liberation may well be the chief limitation of Black Theology. When the immediate concerns of liberation are realized, it is not at all clear where Black Theology is supposed to go."[12] Mbiti incorrectly concludes that Black theology is unfit for Africans and irrelevant for Africa because of his perception of it as hyper-racialized and wrongly fixated on a Western-framed goal of political and economic liberation. He also lamented that Black theology does not emerge from joy, but

---

12. John S. Mbiti, "An African Views American Black Theology," in *Black Theology: A Documentary History*, vol. 1, *1966–1979*, ed. James H. Cone and Gayraud S. Wilmore (Maryknoll, NY: Orbis Books, 1979), 381.

instead "is sorrow, bitterness, anger, and hatred."[13] While the analysis is reductive and perhaps culturally tone-deaf, Mbiti's question about what Black theology looks like after a realized liberation does gesture toward a critique of implicit acceptance of Western/Eurocentric progressivism within its conception of liberation. What happens after liberation is achieved?

The question assumes that liberation is a destination, a goal to which we progress, or toward which we move steadily. Thus, when it is realized, does it make Black theology irrelevant and obsolete? This, in part, is what informed William Jones's hunt for that all-elusive *exultation/liberation event* that would prove that God is in fact on the side of the oppressed and therefore cannot be a white racist. Is liberation reducible to a state of existence achievable when certain conditions are met? And does this understanding of liberation betray a fixation with a temporal orientation? Given the theme of this book, I have to ask what a spatially oriented notion of liberation looks like? Perhaps the telos of traditional Black liberation theology is being described in a way that is overly anthropocentric, such that it fails to account for the Earth and its necessary healing. Mbiti's claim that Black theology derives from feelings of anger and hatred perhaps clumsily alludes to, or is in the same vein as, criticisms leveled at the discourse by both feminist and Womanist scholars as being a function of patriarchy, often accusing it of *Black androcentrism*. Is the preoccupation with liberation a Black male concern rooted in an eagerness for revenge and a desire to usurp white male power, replacing it with Black male power?

Womanist Delores Williams expressly stated that Black theology's goal of liberation was misguided and stemmed from its

13. Mbiti, "African Views American Black Theology," 382.

limited and male-centered conception of the Black experience. For her, Black theology's definition of the Black experience leaves out too much and is fixated on the distorted relationality of Blacks and whites, specifically white men and Black men. According to Cone, the Black experience is "a life of humiliation and suffering … the totality of black existence in a white world where babies are tortured, women are raped and men are shot. The black experience is existence in a system of white racism."[14] What Williams declares is missing is an appreciation of *women's re/production history* which entails acknowledging Black women's ingenuity and ability to create for the survival of the entire family and the community broadly.[15] She is also suggesting that Black male theologians may be plagued with double-consciousness and thus overly fixated with or concerned about the white gaze. She prefers the term *wilderness experience,* a central biblical metaphor and a more expansive term that moves beyond a mere racial analysis to include gender and class. Wilderness also offers a useful metaphor for reminding humans of their relationship to the natural world and the necessity for being in right relationship with the space(s) around them.

For Williams, the goal of liberation in Black theology assumes an "androcentric black history. Therefore a masculine indication of person and masculine models of victimization dominate the language and thought of Black liberation theology."[16] These "masculine models of victimization" leave out Black women's contributions and render invisible the history of their efforts to ensure the survival of the Black family by any means necessary. According to Williams,

    14. Cone, *Black Theology of Liberation*, 23.
    15. Delores S. Williams, *Sisters in the Wilderness: The Challenge of Womanist God-Talk* (Maryknoll, NY: Orbis Books, 1993), 158.
    16. Williams, *Sisters in the Wilderness*, 158.

> Wilderness experience is suggestive of the essential human initiative (along with divine intervention) in the activity of survival, of community building, of structuring a positive quality of life for family and community; it is also suggestive of human initiative in the work of liberation; black experience says very little about black initiative and responsibility in the community's struggle for liberation, and nothing about the internal tensions and intentions in community building and survival struggle.[17]

Additionally, Williams argues that the wilderness experience converges or unites the sacred and secular realities of African American life. It gestures toward a unity of existence that includes the requirement to maintain harmony with the natural world and simultaneously thwarts a zero-sum racial binary that seeks to defeat the oppressor using the oppressor's frame of reference and methods. Thus, Williams suggests that Black theology's conceptualization of liberation perpetuates Black androcentrism.[18]

Womanist theology's shift away from liberation to a theme of survival/improving quality of life is of course explicitly described in Alice Walker's definition of Womanism, as she declared Black women's commitment to the survival of the entire people. Monica Coleman argues that this emphasis on survival/quality of life is not just inherent in what it means to be Womanist but is also tied to Womanist theologians' doctrine of salvation. She describes it as *making a way out of no way.*[19] Coleman summarizes the doctrine of salvation in Womanist

17. Williams, *Sisters in the Wilderness*, 158, 160.
18. Williams, *Sisters in the Wilderness*, 158.
19. Monica Coleman, *Making a Way Out of No Way: A Womanist Theology* (Minneapolis: Fortress Press, 2008), 36.

theology as characteristic of four features: "(1) God's presentation of unforeseen possibilities; (2) human agency; (3) the goal
of justice, survival, and quality of life; and (4) a challenge to
the existing order."[20] She notes that in the writings of Delores
Williams, Kelly Brown Douglas, and Karen Baker Fletcher,
among others, this ethic of survival is a consistent theme. And
while "survival is often inadequate in terms of full liberation,
it is one of the ways in which God saves."[21] Coleman's contribution to this discourse is her timely critique of an exclusively
Christian representation of Womanist theology and her creation
of an alternative, religiously pluralistic version of Womanist theology and soteriology. Her embrace of both Process thought and
African traditional religions, for example, adds complexity to
the conception of salvation/liberation beyond what is possible
within a traditional Western Christian worldview.

For Coleman, Process theology offers a vehicle allowing other
religions to provide resources for the development of Womanist theology and helping to explain and develop the soteriological value of the ethic of survival/quality of life. The idea that
humans have their own self-determining power that God cannot trump or usurp and the idea that the future is open, unde-
termined, and unknown even to God, offering the possibility
for novelty, are key tenets of Process thought. This makes the
possibility of creative transformation the goal and a postmodern
version of *making a way out of no way.* Coleman views liberation
as a term that is both androcentric and anthropocentric. It is
anthropocentric to the extent that it conveys a narrow, human
construction of a utopia that might be inconsistent or out of step
with what God intends.

20. Coleman, *Making a Way*, 33.
21. Coleman, *Making a Way*, 34.

Creative transformation challenges the oppressive forces of society. The aims of creative transformation are particular to each situation, and God may not always lead us in ways that feel liberating. Sometimes the God of creative transformation will feel like a judge. But creative transformation is leading us to a way that will improve quality of life. Creative transformation involves God's presentation of unforeseen possibilities; human agency; a telos of justice, survival, and quality of life; and a challenge to the existing order.[22]

Creative transformation moves beyond the realm of the human and offers soteriological possibilities for the rest of the created order as well. Postmodern Womanist theology, she claims, "will alert African Americans to ecological crises and the notion that the natural world, too, is and must be transformed into a higher quality of its own life. With or without the presence of humanity, God is guiding and transforming the natural world to its best potential as well."[23]

Coleman also uses the telos of creative transformation as a means to incorporate idioms, symbols, and modalities of other religions, particularly African traditional religions. She posits the ancestors not merely as beings from the past but as present, living sources of energy and influence. They help to comprise the power, spirit, and energy of God influencing human beings through dreams, spirit possession, and rememory to work toward survival, improve our quality of life, and creatively transform our present circumstances. Like God, the ancestors' power is noncoercive, luring us to new possibilities for wholeness. Coleman's construction of a postmodern Womanist theol-

---

22. Coleman, *Making a Way*, 93.
23. Coleman, *Making a Way*, 94.

ogy that incorporates Process thought allows for a religiously pluralistic methodology that invites and legitimizes non-Christian, non-Western perspectives. This transforms the conception of telos and view of salvation beyond what is imaginable within an exclusive Western/Eurocentric frame. It means that salvation and/or the telos of liberation cannot be tied only to the nature and structure of the political economy but must also speak to the restoration of the Earth and the reclamation of the land through ecological reparations.

Some Womanists and ecofeminists are taking seriously the need to define survival, wholeness, and ultimate health in planetary terms. Melanie Harris's *Ecowomanism* correctly connects the dots between the history and legacy of white supremacist oppression with the exploitation and destruction of the Earth. She, like Coleman, posits inclusion of African spirituality in what she calls ecowomanist ethics calling for indigenous African and Native American perspectives to be included in cultivation of an ethic for the Earth's healing. Harris posits ecological reparations as part of the process of restoration. Within her formulation, however, it is not clear to me what the practical implications and consequences of this would be. She declares, "Ecological reparations center on repairing ecological violence and recognizing the logic of domination at play in ecocide and genocide—racial, gender, and sexual violence, and ecological violence."[24] But how exactly is this repair of ecological violence accomplished? "Ecological reparations face this truth. To repair acts of violence against Native peoples, and enslaved (or free) African women, we must interrogate the white supremacist mind-set and logic of domination that sits at the root of these structural forms of violence while seeing the impact that this logic of domination also

---

24. Melanie L. Harris, *Ecowomanism: African American Women and Earth-Honoring Faiths* (Maryknoll, NY: Orbis Books, 2017), 144.

has on the Earth."[25] She is correct. I have tried in this work to interrogate whiteness, specifically white epistemological hubris, and its constitutive features of a false universalism, the myth of objectivity, and a vicious individualism. Black and womanist theology have developed as discourses that "interrogate the white supremacist mind-set." The deconstructive work has been done by many. What is less clear is what a constructive theology and program for ecological reparations entails. The question remains: What practical steps must be taken to correct for, and overcome, whiteness? What are ecological reparations, and how do they relate to the previously discussed telos of liberation?

Harris calls for reimagining theology in a way that breaks with dualistic frameworks in Western thought and incorporates more African cosmological logics that convey the importance of interdependence and interconnection. But what are the theological symbols to be reimagined, reinterpreted, or eliminated entirely? And with what should they be replaced? What is called for is a clear theology and pragmatic agenda that will work to ensure robust ecological reparations. I therefore posit ecological reparations as self-conscious acts by which oppressed people reclaim and recover stolen Earth, physical spaces of Earth, and not just farm or green those pieces of land but indigenize/ Africanize those physical spaces. These self-conscious acts of indigenizing space bring together the telos of Black liberation theology with that of ecowomanism and ecotheology generally.

In chapter 2, I argued that the Earth, and the land specifically, should be viewed not as a Western commodity but as a spiritual reality. Based on an indigenous African and Native American perspective, the land has theological meaning and is a theological symbol. It is the home of the ancestors and connects human beings to the rest of the ecosystem. The land/Earth

25. Harris, *Ecowomanism*, 144.

must be reclaimed and restored. A spatially oriented theology calls for a reprioritization of Christian theological symbols in a way that elevates those symbols that promote balance, restoration, and harmony with the space(s) we currently occupy, and diminishes those that reify a past time alienating Christians from present realities. This theological perspective also calls for reimagining our conception of God as the one that fills up the spaces and connects all into a single reality. The cross and the Bible as symbols, because of the legacy of Western, especially Platonic, philosophy, make theology abstract, focused on the distant past, and disconnected from everyday lived realities, particularly those that are related to the legacy of racial injustice and the possibility of planetary disaster. I present the Earth, the land specifically, as a theological symbol that should be elevated above the cross and even the Bible. And the telos of this theology therefore must include some specific claim to land recovery, planetary restoration, and indigenizing/Africanizing specific spaces of Earth. In other words, the goal of liberation must include the Womanist emphasis on survival and wholeness such that it is tied to reclamation of portions of the planet. It is liberation of the land/Earth and those dispossessed from, and spatially confined on, the land/Earth. In this way, ecological reparations would be a tangible and practical goal, a visible representation of spatial healing and recovery.

The land/Earth as theological symbol is not anthropocentric. The focus here is not exclusively that of human concerns, even the concern of oppressed human beings. But this symbol represents the need to bring about balance and harmony with the natural world as much as it does the creation of a political economy intended to correct for past and current racial injustice and gender and class exploitation. The elevation of the land as a theological symbol would require Black churches, and even

Black secular organizations, to engage in projects of land recovery and restoration. For example, the money Black churches raise from tithes and offerings could be used not merely to edify the church itself and its pastor through the building of larger and larger physical church edifices, but also for investing in land purchases both for healthy farming and greening and for indigenizing/Africanizing as acts of ecological repair. Later in the chapter I will examine how the Pan African Orthodox Christian Church and other African-centered groups, like Soul Fire Farms, are making efforts to show how the land/Earth can function as a theological symbol for liberation.

African Ecofeminism and Land Restoration

The emphasis on ecological recovery and land repair ultimately mandates transcending the provincial boundaries of identity established by the modern-day conception of the nation-state. Black and Native Americans' experience of racist land dispossession is not unique to them. This is an experience shared throughout the Third World. Third-World ecofeminists make plain the link between the legacy of European colonialism and ecological devastation. Their work offers insight into the possibility of a Pan-African, or Africana, ecotheology that connects efforts to defeat Western corporate globalization with ecological recovery.

"Green" Christians in Africa, led by ecofeminists, have provided poignant examples of the way restoration of the Earth in response to threats of ecological destruction can fuel and inform Christian faith commitments. Rosemary Radford Ruether, in her explication of the Greening of World Religions, points out the features or ideas of major religions, not just Christianity, that lend themselves to an abuse of nature versus those that are conducive to ecological renewal.

Highly individualistic religious views that concentrate solely on the salvation of the individual "soul" taken out of its social and even corporal contexts are unhelpful. Mandates for unlimited domination that see the (elite male) human as having all power over the rest of nature, and the right to manipulate the rest of nature without regard to its own ecosystems, are problematic. Religions that are highly otherworldly, deeming this world as ephemeral and without intrinsic value, from which the soul should escape to eternal life or await an imminent destruction followed by a heavenly world, are not helpful.[26]

Ruether argues that it is not necessarily the perception that nature is sacred and comprised of deities that leads to ecological sustainability and the process of reversing our march toward ecocide, but rather when religious people recognize that nature has its own integrity and should be respected as self-sustaining. It is when humans accept their limitations and resist overstating their significance and importance to the overall theological design. Humans then need to "actively cultivate respect for nature's own life and see themselves as having to harmonize their own behavior with it.... Human beings are within, not outside of, this self-sustaining ecosystem of the natural world. They can only survive themselves by sustaining it."[27] The works of African ecofeminists reveal the practical tasks that have been performed by Christians who have lived the intersectionality that is the exploitation and oppression of racial/ethnic groups, women, and the Earth.

---

26. Rosemary Radford Ruether, *Integrating Ecofeminism, Globalization, and World Religions* (Lanham, MD: Rowman & Littlefield, 2005), 78.
27. Ruether, *Integrating Ecofeminism*, 79.

Teresia Hinga, a Kenyan ecofeminist, examined the history
of colonialism in Kenya and how it gave birth to an African
women's movement to recover and restore the land. She constructs a "Gikuyu Theology of Land." The precolonial perception of the land, she claims, was predicated on the idea that the
Earth belongs to God alone; thus, no individual can possess or
have absolute ownership of the land. But we all have the responsibility to work on and care for that land. Hinga then explains
how this idea was distorted and damaged by British colonialism. She reveals, "The colonialists introduced the idea that land
was a commodity that could be acquired by the use of money.
This radical commodification of land led to the restriction of
land rights of those who did not have the monetary power in
the society."[28] British colonizers also introduced the idea that
land could be privately held, owned, and restricted by individuals with deeds to that land even if they lived in other countries,
especially the metropole, or homeland of the colonizers, and
did nothing of value with the land. The land essentially became
theirs to squander. Such acts, similar to those performed by
whites in America, led to land dispossession and rigid spatial
confinement of the indigenous people. Additionally, commodi-
fying the land upset the ecological balance, as land was misused
and abused to generate cash crops for profit, degenerating the
soil and heavily relying on chemical fertilizers.[29]

It is in response to this land crisis that women in Kenya have
stepped up to fill the void. In this neocolonial moment, women
have "taken the initiative to fight for land reclamation in both
qualitative and quantitative terms.… Women are forming coop-

28. Teresia Hinga, "The Gikuyu Theology of Land and Environmental
Justice," in *Women Healing Earth: Third World Women on Ecology, Feminism,
and Religion*, ed. Rosemary Radford Ruether (Maryknoll, NY: Orbis Books,
1996), 180.
29. Hinga, "Gikuyu Theology of Land," 177.

eratives to buy land, to build and improve their homes, to construct dams and water tanks to collect rain water, and even to
pay school fees for their children."[30] Additionally, the Green
Belt Movement, founded by a feminist ecologist, began mobiliz-
ing women around aggressive campaigns to reforest sections of
Kenya. "The organization aims not only at reclaiming the quality of the land through planting trees, it also aims at reclaiming
women's power by planting afresh the sense of self-confidence
and pride in themselves nurtured in precolonial times by many
African societies."[31] Hinga's theology of land helps transform
African women's perception both of the land and of themselves, reminding them that the Earth is here for our mutual
sustenance, not a possession to be weaponized and wielded over
others as a mechanism of domination or exercise of wealth and
material excess.

Similarly, ecofeminists in South Africa describe the same
phenomenon, a history of land dispossession followed by postcolonial efforts to reclaim and restore the land. Denise Ackerman and Tahira Joyner are particularly attentive to the role that
African Initiated Churches (AICs) play in leading these efforts
at ecological restoration. She describes tree-planting campaigns
by AICs in Zimbabwe, where the churches have been intentional
about preaching and teaching a salvation that is connected to
the entire created order. "In declaring the so-called 'war of the
trees' an ecumenical platform was created in order to unite the
churches in a green army and to launch environmental reform
in terms of creation's liberation."[32] The idea of liberation for
all creation necessarily changes the conventional definition of

---

30. Hinga, "Gikuyu Theology of Land," 182.

31. Hinga, "Gikuyu Theology of Land," 182.

32. Denise Ackerman and Tahira Joyner, "Earth-Healing in South
Africa," in Ruether, *Women Healing Earth*, 126.

"liberation" beyond a mere anthropocentric discussion of political economy to one that also includes land renewal, recovery, and restoration. According to Ackerman and Joyner, "Prophets are turning their healing colonies into 'environmental hospitals' in which the patient is the denuded earth, the 'dispensary' is the nursery where the correct medicine is being prepared, and the community is the healing agent."[33] The greening of Christianity happens when African, or so-called Third World, eco-feminist women lead, since their lived experiences reside at the intersection of these concerns. Postcolonial African women's perspectives help lay the foundation for a Pan-African spatial theology of land/Earth healing, recovery, and restoration. Their acts of ingenuity are birthed by necessity as women work to *make a way out of no way* in order to save the community and even the Earth itself.

A spatially oriented telos of liberation manifests land recovery, revitalization, and ecological healing. In many ways, this perspective harks back to twentieth-century African American varieties of Black nationalism often centered on securing land in order to establish a Black nation-state. This nation-state would consist of independent institutions that Black people owned and controlled. Malcolm X often proclaimed, "A revolution is based on land. Land is the basis of all independence. Land is the basis of freedom, justice, and equality."[34] While many Black Nationalist frameworks have been appropriately criticized for their sexist, masculinist conceptions of leadership, heterosexism, and problematic Western assumptions about the value of the nation-state model, it is worth examining their efforts at land sovereignty so as to learn the lessons of their successes and failures.

33. Ackerman and Joyner, "Earth-Healing in South Africa," 127.
34. Malcolm X, "Message to the Grassroots," speech delivered in Detroit, Michigan, December 1963.

Marcus Garvey's Universal Negro Improvement Association (UNIA) and his *Back to Africa* program sought to secure land in Liberia for African Americans and to fund these efforts through investments in Black-owned businesses and financial interests in commercial boats like the Black Star Line. The UNIA also purchased a farm in Liberty, Ohio, around 1945.[35] The Nation of Islam (NOI), under the leadership of Elijah Muhammad, at its peak in the late 1960s owned approximately 13,000 acres of farmland in Georgia and Alabama. After the decline and fracturing of NOI after the death of Elijah Muhammad, it lost and/or had dissolved much of these assets, yet the organization tried again, in 1994, to reinvest in land, creating Muhammad Farms on 1,556 acres in rural Georgia.[36] Both examples describe efforts that were plagued by mismanagement, a Western, patriarchal hierarchy, and a religious orientation that failed to connect indigenous African and Native American spirituality to land recovery. Land was primarily conceptualized as a vehicle for farming in order to feed the Black masses and establish Black independence.

However, there have been alternative models. Fannie Lou Hamer's Freedom Farm Cooperative (FFC) is one such example. Hamer established the farm through the collective pooling of resources as a survival instrument through which the Black community in the poorest areas in Mississippi in Sunflower County could feed themselves and then be empowered for political activism. Hamer adeptly connected Black people's lack of control of the land to the very real possibility of starvation in that rural county in Mississippi. So poor Black people's ability

---

35. Monica M. White, *Freedom Farmers: Agricultural Resistance and the Black Freedom Movement* (Chapel Hill: University of North Carolina Press, 2019), 16.

36. White, *Freedom Farmers*, 18.

to feed themselves was not only a survival necessity but also a mechanism toward political empowerment. Monica White asserts, "Fannie Lou Hamer emphasizes that the leverage of owning land and the fact that land supports people have given those people a wedge into the political machine—rich, white, and racist—that has always run Mississippi."[37] Hamer clearly saw Black land ownership and its cultivation not merely as a way to provide much-needed food to stave off possible starvation, but also viewed the land as a vehicle for liberation. According to White,

> In creating Freedom Farm, Hamer intended to concentrate on three primary areas: (1) building affordable, clean, and safe housing; (2) creating an entrepreneurial clearinghouse—a small business incubator that would provide resources for new business owners and retraining for those with limited educational skills but with agricultural knowledge and manual labor experience; and (3) developing an agricultural cooperative that would meet the food and nutritional needs of the county's most vulnerable.[38]

Freedom Farm was a 692-acre farm cooperatively owned and worked by about 1,500 people in rural Mississippi. After some very successful years employing over forty people, housing seventy-three families, and feeding thousands of families through subsistence crops, the FFC ran into trouble when several tornadoes hit Sunflower County in 1971. In 1972 and 1973, droughts and then floods destroyed crops, and disaster relief consumed the operating budget. White benefactors began to

---

37. White, *Freedom Farmers*, 71.
38. White, *Freedom Farmers*, 72.

withdraw their support, making the FFC unable to pay its mort-
gages, and it eventually began to sell off its land to pay back state
and county taxes. These deathblows also unfortunately coin-
cided with the declining health of Fannie Lou Hamer. While
certainly short-lived, the FFC established an example of cooperative land ownership that offered a glimpse of the possibilities for
addressing issues related to the lack of housing, unemployment,
the problem of miseducation, and a lack of access to nutritional
foods. It presented a model of the land/Earth as both symbol of
and vehicle for salvation/liberation. As a 1968 report on self-help
campaigns summarized, "the important part is that the people
themselves have a stake in it; they are not relying on hand-outs;
they are enhancing their own dignity and freedom by learning
that they can feed themselves through their own efforts."[39] Fannie Lou Hamer's Freedom Farm Cooperative not only exem-
plified how land is instrumental to political liberation but also
offered a glimpse of what ecological reparations could be.

Practical Efforts at African-Centered Land Recovery in the Twenty-First Century

The Pan African Orthodox Christian Church (PAOCC), also
known as the Shrine of the Black Madonna, founded by Albert
B. Cleage Jr., one of the original architects of Black liberation
theology, was intended to embody the principles of Black Power
and Black Nationalism. Inspired by Marcus Garvey's UNIA
and the Nation of Islam, the PAOCC also established a farm
and land recovery project called the Beulah Land Farms. From
1980 to 1999, the church under Cleage's leadership raised over
ten million dollars to purchase and help build the infrastructure
for over four thousand acres of land in Calhoun Falls, South

39. White, *Freedom Farmers*, 75.

Carolina. The purchase and investment in this land, intended to be the first of many Beulah Lands, represented a philosophical and programmatic shift in Cleage's thinking following the end of the Black Power movement, or the Black revolution. Cleage evolved his perspective from one in which the goal was immediate revolutionary action and political liberation to the creation of a sustainable transforming community that could become an enclave of survival, wholeness, and protection with Beulah Land at the center.

In the mid-1960s, Cleage described his Black Christian Nationalist movement (BCN) as one intended to bring about the liberation of Black people with the church as the vehicle for that liberation. He proclaimed from his pulpit in Detroit, Michigan, "Nothing is more sacred than the liberation of Black people," and he called upon the church to radically change its theology and program in order to make it an effective instrument for Black liberation. He taught that Jesus was a revolutionary Black messiah, a leader trying to liberate his people from white Roman oppression in the first century, and that Jesus's struggle is the same struggle as Black peoples' in America in the 1960s. Cleage's interpretation of the gospel made the Shrine of the Black Madonna the home for young Black Power activists like Stokely Carmichael (a.k.a. Kwame Ture), who coined the term "Black Power." However, as the fervor of the Black Power movement began to wane and a forty-year white political backlash slowly deteriorated the achievements of the civil rights movement and ushered in an era of mass incarceration, Cleage evolved his position and program. He too began to redefine liberation in a way that needed to take into account what womanists stress as an emphasis on survival, wholeness, and quality of life. He began to reconceptualize liberation away from its emphasis on a temporal, progressive destination to one that considers the requirement to reclaim the land and restore lost spaces. He wanted to create enclaves of consciousness and communal living. Cleage shifts from a focus on revolution to a focus on radical transformation, what Coleman calls *creative transformation.* As early as 1978, Cleage understood that:

> The Black revolution has just about run out of gas. We have to start planning for survival. The factories are being automated with robots and computers.… Unskilled black people in America are going to be economically obsolete. That means the cities will become cesspools of crime, drugs, poverty and violence. We could offer an alternative to that life by building communal Christian communities that would provide a safe haven. BCN must be a refuge and a hope for black people intelligent enough to seek it. We have to preserve what we have built by institutionalizing it in the clothing of the church.… WE have to focus on transformation rather than revolution.[40]

Cleage's evolved theology and conception of God as cosmic energy and creative intelligence helped him appreciate the connection between the exploitation, and now economic obsolescence, of Black people and the exploitation of the Earth. The communal enclaves he sought to create would also be ecological reformation projects. Salvation for Black people therefore lay in restoring the land/Earth as a refuge from the vestiges of whiteness, specifically its vicious individualism.

> Human society cannot survive without a conscious restructuring of its basic foundations. Total commit-

---

40. Albert Cleage, unpublished sermon discussion, Shrine #10, Houston, Texas, 1998.

ment to communalism as a way of life and acceptance of the Unified Field concept of God's power are essential cornerstones of the new order. We recognize individualism as a global cancer that has infected and contaminated the whole of human life. Everywhere there are inescapable signs of impending disaster. Ecological dangers can no longer be dismissed as the cult fact of flower children living beyond their time. Nuclear and chemical contamination threaten the very existence of human life on the planet, where man has poisoned the air, the earth, and the fresh water supply. Gradually we are coming to realize that as important as these problems are, they are only symptoms of an underlying global sickness rooted deep in an individualistic human psyche.[41]

As part of this ecological recovery, in the waning years of his life Cleage and his church purchased over four thousand acres of land in Abbeville, South Carolina. The land is in part a farm and also a resource for housing, educational institutions, conference centers, recreation, a water-bottling facility, and spiritual retreats. Its restoration is also a quintessential illustration of ancestral remembrance and the reclamation of stolen Earth marked by the death of Anthony Crawford.

In 1916, Anthony Crawford owned 429 acres of land, inherited from his father, just outside of Abbeville, South Carolina. On October 21, 1916, when a disagreement with a white store owner over the cost of cottonseed escalated, Crawford was assaulted by an employee of the store. Soon a white mob began to form and Crawford was arrested in part for his own protec-

41. Albert Cleage, "Genesis II: The Re-Creation of Man," unpublished article, 1984.

tion. Upon his release, however, he was eventually cornered by the white mob, stabbed, beaten, and ultimately lynched from a tree. His body was then shot repeatedly. The local newspaper's headline the next day read, "Negro Strung Up and Shot to Pieces."[42] A year later, in October 1917, in a community meeting in Abbeville courthouse, the town voted to expel Crawford's family from the community, and his land and property holdings were seized. Additionally, all Black businesses in Abbeville were shutdown. Black land/Earth was stolen through heinous violence, the negative energy of which was subsumed by the land; thus, the purchase of Beulah Land by the PAOCC, almost a century later, represents an act of spiritual, ancestral, and ecological recovery and repair. It is an act of ritual cleansing and redemption designed both to reclaim Black spaces and to restore balance and harmony with the Earth, the ecosystem. Cleage envisioned Beulah Land as a Black self-determination project and as a refuge from a neoliberal system moving so many Black and brown people toward economic obsolescence.

Under the current regional bishop, Rev. D. Kimathi Nelson, the plan is for Beulah Land to offer a full and bountiful existence. Nelson stated, "the last 15 years were a struggle to hold on to the land since its purchase in 2000."[43] This was due to vicious opposition within the USDA, banks, and the surrounding community in rural South Carolina who both objected to and put up obstacles in front of a Black church engaging in farming on this large a scale. However, Nelson notes, "the problem has now been solved. The land is ours. Now we must build up the infrastructure and establish an anchor business."[44] According to Nelson,

42. "Anthony Crawford, a Negro of Wealth, Lynched Saturday," *Abbeville Press and Banner*, Abbeville, South Carolina, October 25, 1917.

43. Interview with Rev. D. Kimathi Nelson, June 2021.

44. Interview with Rev. D. Kimathi Nelson, June 2021.

there are many projects being developed, from cattle farming to solar farming and plant medicine. There are also several fresh-water wells on the property, which will enable the establishment of a bottled water company. The land already currently hosts summer camps where children are educated in Black history, the need for food sovereignty, and African-centered spirituality. Plans are underway to develop affordable housing on the land and several homes have already been constructed.

As the regional bishop, Nelson is first and foremost a pastor and theologian. He often explains Beulah Land as a theological concept and symbol, preaching that Beulah Land is not a single place but a theological idea. It represents land/Earth, a place of refuge intended to offer a countercultural and alternate world-view to the one predicated on capitalism, neoliberal values, and individualism. It reimagines land/Earth as owned by God and cooperatively shared by a group of people, a place of reconnec-tion where humans are reminded of their purpose and the need to maintain balance and harmony within an ecosystem. Nelson makes clear that the idea is to replicate Beulah Land throughout the African diaspora, in North America, the Caribbean, and Africa. The PAOCC has already established a branch in Liberia, West Africa, and plans to create the next Beulah Land on the African continent. These various locations serve as ecological land recovery and Black self-determination projects, designed both to secure Black survival, to improve the quality of life, and to offer ritual cleansing and healing for the death, exploitation, and harm committed on and to these pieces of Earth. Beulah Lands constitute liberated zones, spaces of refuge and protec-tion from the violence and death that stalk Black existence in the aftermath of slavery in the Western world. Beulah Lands offer a counter to the nihilism of Afropessimists by construct-ing new Christian symbols that prioritize recovered land/Earth as theological act. Black salvation and healing lie in the blood-soaked land/Earth, the place of ancestral redemption, not escape from the Earth for some imagined heaven after death. Nor does salvation lie exclusively in a political economy, even a democratic socialist one, if the Earth is burning all around us. Such acts of land recovery offer postmodern examples of Christian works that lay the foundation for a more pluralistic approach to religious faith.

Soul Fire Farm

There are other models of land recovery, farming, and spatial healing in the United States that expressly embrace traditional African religions in their efforts at farming and ecological recovery. Soul Fire Farm is an Afro-Indigenous centered community farm working to feed people, mostly Black and brown, in the greater Albany, New York, area who suffer from food scarcity and live in food-apartheid communities. Soul Fire farming practices center on honoring the spirits of the land and discerning spiritual intentionality for these pieces of Earth by pouring libations to ancestors and engaging in divination. They have cultivated farming practices from African cultures, such as the raised-bed practice of the Ovambo people of Northern Namibia, in an effort to restore degraded soil and decrease soil erosion. Through this and other African spiritual farming practices, they have been able to regenerate eighty acres of mountainside land. Their ancestral farming practice "concentrates fertile topsoil, aerates soil, and prevents waterlogging."[45] The farm manager is an initiated priestess and Queen Mother

---

45. Leah Penniman, *Farming While Black: Soul Fire Farm's Practical Guide to Liberation on the Land* (White River Junction, VT: Chelsea Green Publishing, 2018), 75.

in the Vodun/Vodou religion, which incorporates divination, spirit possession, and dream interpretation as modes of communication with the invisible, spiritual entities on the land they occupy.[46] In her work *Farming While Black,* Leah Penniman recounts an episode in which she received a message from spirit via a dream. The message required her to inquire as to the motives of some of the visitors to the land and root out the arrogance and negative energy perceived by the spirits of the land. Penniman informed the vistors that they would all need to make a cornmeal offering to Akaka, spirit of agriculture, in order to mitigate the discomfort.[47]

These traditional African spiritual modalities, practiced in the twenty-first century, provide a mechanism through which this community simultaneously accomplishes its task of feeding food-insecure people while maintaining balance and harmony with the larger ecosystem and the invisible spiritual realm. Soul Fire Farm embodies fully the practice, not merely of greening the land/space in response to the urgency of climate change, but of indigenizing/Africanizing their space(s), which is the repudiation of whiteness and brings about the healing of the Earth. Both Beulah Land and Soul Fire Farm offer examples of Black people engaging in practical efforts to connect theology to land recovery and exemplify what ecological reparations could mean as well as the practice of reclaiming and indigenizing stolen Earth.

Conclusion

This chapter has sought to interrogate the telos of liberation in Black theology in order to distill some of its underlying assumptions and present an alternative conception rooted in a

---

46. Penniman, *Farming While Black*, 54.
47. Penniman, *Farming While Black*, 60.

spatial orientation. Early critics of Black theology forced it to investigate some of the bourgeois assumptions in the definition of liberation suggesting that Black theology might be informed by a middle-class consciousness. Since his first book, James Cone has asserted a difference between revolution and protest. "Revolution sees every particular wrong as one more instance in a pattern which is itself beyond rectification. Revolution aims at the substitution of a new system for one adjudged to be corrupt, rather than corrective adjustments within the existing system."[48] The question has always been, however, what is the exact nature of this new system? Cornel West and Cone both believe that Marxist analysis should be used to critique the individualism and greed that rest at the heart of capitalism and neoliberalism. Capitalism should be replaced with some form of democratic socialism. Black people need to have influence over the means of production and address the core issue of Black economic powerlessness. Latin American (male) liberation theologians drew some of the same conclusions given that their use of the term *liberation* was explicitly conceptualized solely in economic terms as a reaction to Western globalization. They were reacting specifically against the Western theory of development with which "underdeveloped" countries in Latin America were beset.

While my argument does not disagree with the promotion of democratic socialism, something is missing if the contours of liberation are confined solely to various forms of the political economy. Doing this limits our conceptualization of the term in a way that is excessively anthropocentric. What is missing is consideration of the Earth and how liberation must also take into consideration the problem of impending ecocide and the

48. James H. Cone, *Black Theology and Black Power*, 50th anniversary ed. (Maryknoll, NY: Orbis Books, 2018), 136.

legacy of racist land dispossession. Liberation should not be understood solely within a Eurocentric temporal conceptualization of progress, which too often reduces the Earth to just another commodity, a component within the Eurocentric technological order, an object alongside Black, brown, and indigenous people.

First-generation Womanist religious scholars describe this limitation in Black theology as attributable to *Black androcentrism*; thus, this theology evinces a Black patriarchal perspective rooted in Black male victimization. Drawing from Alice Walker's definition, the Womanist perspective seeks to focus on the goal of survival, wholeness, and improving the quality of life. Monica Coleman would describe this as consistent with the Black church mantra of *making a way out of no way.* She uses Process thought to argue that creative transformation might be a more apt teleological emphasis than liberation. Creative transformation allows space for novelty, for unknown possibilities to emerge that defy human limitations and expectations. As such it is a term that implicitly critiques the anthropocentric nature of Black (and brown) male frameworks of liberation. Ultimately, land/Earth will play a role in what creative transformation will be.

Womanists and African feminists offer an intersectional analysis that has been more likely to include the problem of ecocide and the exploitation of the Earth. Melanie Harris's call for ecological reparations must be considered in the context of the telos of Black theology. Her framing of ecological reparations asks us to consider liberation more within the framework of African spirituality in a way that promotes the interdependency and interconnection of all reality. It demands that we take seriously the role humans must play in maintaining a balanced cosmic order.

I argue that the demand for ecological reparations needs to be explained in pragmatic and practical terms for theology and its telos. Liberation has to include a process of land recovery, healing, and renewal. It has to be tied to ancestral rememory and to account for blood-soaked portions of the Earth where lives and land were stolen due to vicious white supremacist violence. Fannie Lou Hamer understood this well. Her Freedom Farm Cooperative was an idea developed out of desperate necessity as Black people in rural, racist Mississippi were confronted with the very real prospect of starvation. Though ultimately unsuccessful and short-lived, Hamer's Freedom Farm Cooperative was fashioned based on an African-centered vision of land as cooperatively owned and developed. It offered a model of land recovery as space for Black survival and refuge from a racist society that merged the concern for political liberation with ecological repair.

The Pan African Orthodox Christian Church (a.k.a. The Shrine of the Black Madonna) currently has a program for liberation tied to land recovery and restoration in the spirit of Hamer's Freedom Farm. The PAOCC, formerly Black Christian Nationalism, is no longer a revolutionary movement focused on the dismantling and deconstruction of Western society so much as it is now an attempt to create transforming communities, across national boundaries, enclaves of refuge, healing, restoration, and recovery ultimately intended to address Black economic powerlessness, creating a path for Black control of the means of production, and, at the same time, restoring ecological balance and harmony with the rest of the created order. Beulah Land exemplifies ecological repair, addressing the need for food sovereignty, providing an economic engine, offering protection from an antiblack society, and incorporating an African-centered understanding of Earth reminding human beings of their proper relationship to the Earth and its needed mainte-nance.

Soul Fire Farm, even more explicitly than Cleage's church, engages in African farming and spiritual practices both to feed Black and brown people who suffer from food insecurity and to replenish degraded soil and trap carbon dioxide in order to contribute to the healing of the ecosphere.

The PAOCC's Beulah Land farms and Soul Fire Farm both provide a model of indigenizing/Africanizing space as a form of liberation. Both offer a vision of liberation that is transcontextual in that it attempts to transverse the limits that bind identity to the nation-state. African descendants of slaves in America are not some special, uniquely oppressed group separate and distinct from continental and other diasporic Africans. Continental and diasporic Africans have the same history of land dispossession and are often the most vulnerable to the destruction waged by climate change, or ecocide. This is why the work of African eco-feminists provides a necessary framework and practices toward land restoration. Thus, what is actually being proposed is a type of Pan-African, or Africana, ecotheology predicated on land recovery rooted in an African-centered theological conception of land/Earth that prioritizes space over time considerations. The Earth cries out for healing from the wages of white episte-mological hubris, and the land remains soaked with the blood of Black people's and Native Americans' ancestors, whose death led to vicious land dispossession that continues to demand an accounting. Rituals of libation pouring, spirit possession, and even divination offer modalities through which descendants can connect with the land and their ancestors, encourage reciprocity, and restore and remember what has been stolen and forgotten.

Index

Ackerman, Denise, 182
African Initiated Churches (AICs), 182–83
African mysticism
 and doctrine of God, 105
 as source for theology, 113–14, 122–23
 See also Black religion; spirituality, African
African spirituality. *See* spirituality, African
African traditional religion: and liberation theology, 45–46
Africana ecotheology, 38
 predicated on land recovery, 197
Africana theological methodology, x, xxii–xxiv, 1–36, 87–88, 113
Afropessimism/Afropessimists, xviii, 128
 and Black social death, xxviii
 of Black theology and Black churches, 134
 and society's view of Black people, 163–64
 and symbols of cross and Bible, 125–26
 and violence, 134
AICs. *See* African Initiated Churches
Alexander, Michelle, 62
ancestor(s)
 African understanding of, 44–45
 as alternative symbols, 142–48
 as category of meaning, 124–25, 143
 and idea of death, 147
 and land/Earth, xix, xxiv, 61, 125, 160–61

linking racial suffering to Earth's suffering, 143, 145–46
 as living reality and metaphor, 145–46
 as present, contemporaneous realities, 43, 44, 148
 reconceptualization of Black life and, 143
 as theological symbol, xxviii, xxix, 125–26, 144–148
 transcending limits of blackness, 160–61
Anderson, Victor, 94
Ani, Marimba, 162–63
apartheid in South Africa, xxv, 73

Bailey, Randall, xxix, 156–58
Barth, Karl, 12–13
BCN. *See* Black Christian Nationalist movement
Beulah Land Farms, 186–87
 as model of indigenizing/ Africanizing space, 197
 as theological concept and symbol, 191–92
Bible
 as cultural tool, 151–52
 as disconnected from everyday realities, 178
 double-consciousness and, 160
 as ethically ambivalent, 150
 idea of election in, 120, 156–57
 as idol, 149
 overdependence on, 19–23
 as religious symbol, 148–59
 as source for theology, 149–50, 159
 spatial reading of, 155–56

198

subversive reading of, 157–58
viewed as objective source of truth, 160
as "Word of God," xxi, xvii, 149–50, 159
See also scripture
bibliolatry, 7–8
Black androcentrism, 171, 195
Black Christian Nationalist Manifesto, 108–9
Black Christian Nationalist movement (BCN), 187–88
Black churches, 57–58
Black Consciousness Movement, xxv, 73
Black faith: as different from white faith, 20–21
Black liberation theology
critical of neoliberalism, 163–64
critiques of, xi
deriving from Black experience, ix
goal and methodology of, 164
and reclaiming of stolen spaces, xv
telos of, xv, xxix–xxx, 162, 163–64, 177
and white epistemological hubris, xv
See also liberation; liberation theologies
Black Nationalism: and reclamation of land, 183–84
Black Panther Party: embrace of Marxism by, 167
Black people
as aftermath property, 137
alienated from their own spaces, 27
assimilation of, to American Protestant worldview, 48–49
citizenship of, in global terms, 129
failed by Christianity, 127–28
involuntary presence of in America, 47–48
as no-citizens, 137
Black Power movement, 135; and Black liberation theology, ix
Black religion: white denigration of, 29–31

See also African mysticism; spirituality, African
Black religious experience, 46–47
Black social death. *See* social death, xxvii
Black suffering. *See* suffering, Black
Black theology
Black androcentrism in, 164
and Christian apologetics, 99
and double-consciousness, 107, 121–23
early bourgeois assumptions of, 194
ecological implications of, x
and fetishism of revelation, 93–101
and "freedom of interpretation," 160
infected with whiteness, xxvi
lack of social theory in, 165–66
liberation and, xxi (*see also* Black liberation theology; liberation)
maintaining Christian bona fides, 94
new categories needed for, 31–36
as practiced in West, xi, 5
as revolutionary praxis, 105
and second-sight, 88–93
Black women: invisibilization of, 20
blackness
ontological, 94, 122–23
as oppressed existence, 163
Blake, Jacob, 137
Bletcher, Karen Baker, 174
Boulaga, Eboussi
on Christianities, 90
on fetish, 92
on fetishism of revelation, 88
on fetishization of biblical conception of God, 100
on overreliance on Western theology, xxvi–xxvii
on Western missionary view of revelation as fetish religion, 90–91
Brown, Ras Michael, 50–51
Bultmann, Rudolf, 12
Butler, Jon, 30

Gebara, Ivone
  holistic and affective epistemology
    of, 32–33
  on problem of essentialist
    epistemology, 23–25
Ghana, xxi–xxii, 64–67
globalization
  effects of, in Africa, 65–66
  and private property, 40–41
God, God concept, God-symbol
  of African mysticism, 82
  as agential Supreme Being, 102,
    118
  anthropomorphic conception of, 83
  of classical theism, 82–83
  as cosmic energy, 110–11, 188
  as creative energy, power, and
    intelligence, 35–36, 113–14,
    122–23
  and double-consciousness, 118–19
  and ecotheology, 102–5
  freedom of, 36
  Pan-African conception of, 82–123
  pantheistic conception of, xviii–xx,
    102
  reimagining of, 178
  religion and, 116–17
  on side of oppressed, 94–101
  spatial conception of, xxvii–xxviii,
    113–15
  and temporal orientation, 13,
    82–83
  as unifying power, 87–88
Gramsci, Antonio, 106–7
Great Migration: and spatial
    alienation, 61–62

Ham, curse of, 150–52
Hamer, Fannie Lou, 184–86, 196
Harris, Cheryl, 17
Harris, Melanie, 176–77
hegemony: Gramscian category of,
    105–7
Hilson, Eli, 56
Hinga, Teresia, 181–82
Holmes, William F., 56
Hopkins, Samuel, 150–51

Hose, Sam, 128
housing projects: and spatial
    containment, 62
Hucks, Tracey, xi, 8–9

imperialism/imperialists
  continuing land theft by, 59
  ecological, 29
  as field of knowledge, 93, 112–13
  impacts of, 27, 64
  and land dispossession in Africa,
    xxv, 37–81
  and white supremacy, 27
indigenous African religions:
    understanding of conjure in,
    35–36
individualism
  glorification of, 163
  as result of Enlightenment, xvi
  and white epistemological hubris,
    xv, 177

Jaspin, Elliot, 57
Jesus Christ, 95
  execution of, and lynching, 129–30
  as hero ancestor, 148–49
  as revolutionary Black messiah,
    187
Jim Crow era, xxiv, xxviii
Johnson, Elizabeth A.
  on conversion and ecocide, 77–79
  elements of hubris manifested by,
    79–81
  theocentric view of the world of,
    80–81
  on traditional Catholic theology
    and ecological destruction,
    77–78
Johnson, Sylvester, 91, 150
Jones, William
  on Black suffering, 106, 133
  on Black theology, xxvii
  debate with Albert Cleague Jr., 117
  debate with James Cone, 94–101
  and search for liberation event, 171
  and theological method, 97–98
Joyner, Tahira, 182